MODERN KNIFE COMBAT

THE TRAINING OF A KNIFE FIGHTER

Written in memory of my friend, Sifu Ernie Franco, whose skill with the defensive edge was always tempered with a good heart and best intentions.

MODERN KNIFE COMBAT

THE TRAINING OF A KNIFE FIGHTER

Greg Walker

Paladin Press
Boulder, Colorado

Also by Greg Walker:

Battle Blades: A Professional's Guide to Combat/Fighting Knives

Modern Knife Combat: The Training of a Knife Fighter
by Greg Walker

Copyright © 1995 by Greg Walker

ISBN 0-87364-849-8
Printed in the United States of America

Published by Paladin Press, a division of
Paladin Enterprises, Inc., P.O. Box 1307,
Boulder, Colorado 80306, USA.
(303) 443-7250

Direct inquiries and/or orders to the above address.

CONTENTS

ATTRIBUTES OF THE MODERN BLADESMAN

Deception
The Element of Surprise

Adaptability
Going with the Battle's Flow

Visual Perception
Seeing the Unseen

Guts
The Core Element of Courage

Aggressiveness
"Just Win, Baby"

Emotional Detachment
Professionalism

Pain Acceptance
Both Giving and Taking Thereof

Attack Line Familiarization
Making the Hit

***

Restraint and Mercy
What Separates Man from Animal

WARNING

The techniques and drills depicted in this book are extremely dangerous. Knife training is inherently hazardous and must be undertaken with the proper safety procedures and devices. The reader is strongly advised to seek out certified professional training and instruction before attempting any techniques or drills depicted in this book.

The author, publisher, and distributors of this book disclaim any liability from any damage or injuries that a user of this book may suffer, as well as any liability from any damage or injuries to third parties from the user of this book. This book is presented *for academic study only*.

PREFACE

"The blade arts must not be confused. They are not a sports game! It is about life and death! When you look at a blade on the flow of traditional angles, the movements are very beautiful. Once they are used in actual combat or in use for real, they turn dark, very dark. It could be a very beautiful art, if you look at it that way. Just hope that you don't have to use it or call on the dark side."

Guro Sonny Umpad
Full Contact, February 1995

Although it might seem logical that a book on knife combatives would follow my first book, *Battle Blades: A Professional's Guide to Combat/Fighting Knives*, the decision to produce such a text was not easy. Writing about knives is far easier than learning how to employ them properly in either self-defense or combat, and to address the subject of knife fighting, I needed to make a commitment to the arts as a practitioner, not an observer.

In doing so over the two years it has taken to research this effort, I have been privileged to learn from a cadre of truly exceptional teachers. This book, then, is not about my expertise in the field of knife combatives but about theirs. Let there be no doubt that my military background in special operations as well as editor's role at both *Fighting Knives* and *Full Contact* magazines prepared me for such instruction. It did, and in fact allowed many doors to be opened that were normally reserved for advanced students of the knife. I am honored to be so recognized by those who have been or remain today my teachers.

The primary truth in blade combatives is this. You cannot hope to author a book on the subject unless you have accepted the responsibility to train in the art. To ingest books, magazine articles, and video programs on knife fighting only stimulates the intellectual side of the house. Such resources are wonderful as data bases, *but they cannot replicate actual physical training in the use of the knife as a means of self-defense.*

In developing this book, I sought to approach knife fighting from two distinct and important perspectives. The first was as a potentially lethal means of protecting either myself or my family in a manner which was both discriminating and skillful. Anyone can take a craft or art and debase it to the point where even the most mediocre practitioner is proficient. Certainly the blade arts have experienced such treatment in modern times, as any number of texts and video "slash and dash" programs attest to. Approached from a higher value standard, however, knife training for self-defense truly becomes an art form. As such, it demands self-discipline, physical sacrifice, and hours of study in order to refine one's mental, emotional, spiritual, and physical attributes.

My second goal was to present a book that was both a chronicle of my own experiences as a student of the knife arts as well as a guidebook the reader could actually learn from. Past books on the subject, although perhaps well researched and written, fall short of encouraging the reader to pursue actual training on the physical level. The flow of information on attack angles, footwork, grip styles, and lethal/nonlethal target zones is as impressive as it is repetitive in most recently published texts. Added to this is the tendency of many authors to adopt a specific fighting art as their own, thereby taking a position of expertise which often bars consideration of other arts and practitioners for whom the knife is equally important.

Modern Knife Combat seeks only to apply more than 20 years of personal experience as a law enforcement officer, professional soldier, executive protection specialist, and writer to realistic self-defense using edged steel. If this book is a tribute to anyone, then I propose due accolades belong to those men and women who have devoted their lives to the martial arts, specifically those centered on man's oldest tool/weapon. It was them who I turned to for guidance and they who have taught me more than simply how to wield a blade in proper fashion.

It is my sincere hope the reader will be encouraged by what is to follow. We live in a world that offers little in terms of personal security. Law enforcement can do little to protect you and me before the fact, and the courts today offer us sad recourse if and when a violator is brought before the judge. The threat of acute violence is real and exists in our neighborhoods, workplaces, and across our borders whenever we travel for business or pleasure. Self-protection by means of self-defense is an act of individual survival as well as a personal responsibility.

A knife in the hands of a trained, socially responsible individual can make and has made the difference between life or death. Today's world is weapons-inclined, meaning an emphasis on empty-hand self-defense is as foolish as it is ineffective when we are faced with a real-world assault. Knife combatives training is a war art, not a sporting event or new age evolution of feel-good martial artware. Applied knowledge in the use of the knife translates as personal power over those who would make us their victims. It is for this reason alone that I have elected to add my own experiences in such combatives to your library.

THE MILITARY
FIGHTING SYSTEM

CHAPTER ONE

"During knife fighting, you must eliminate the opponent in the most ruthless and violent manner possible . . . The knife is plunged repeatedly into the opponent until he is destroyed."

Close Combat, FMFM 0-7
U.S. Marine Corps, 09 July 1993

It was the following mind-set I brought to *Fighting Knives* magazine in 1988 and why the late Ernie Franco was invited to write "Street Sense," our first column on edged self-defense. "The civilian will want to use *only* that much more force than his attacker is using against him," offered Franco in his first column. "Once your adversary cannot continue his attack upon you—run, walk, or call the nearest law enforcement agency."

Clearly the civilian is mandated to defend himself under far different constraints than the combat soldier, whose job is essentially offensive in both training and war fighting. The infantryman or special operations soldier is groomed to close with the enemy by force of arms and destroy him, period.

Please note the distinction made between those soldiers whose primary military occupational specialty is war fighting and those who support the war fighters. The difference between these two groups lies in their mental/emotional/spiritual/physical preparation by the military. Combat troops are trained to do but one thing: kill the enemy. Support troops support the professional killers. In today's army, for example, there are more than 1.1 million support personnel but only 50,000 "trigger pullers."

Nearly every U.S. text on knife fighting published during the last half century leans heavily on a military combatives foundation. Enormous credit is given to Col. Rex Applegate (Ret.), Lt. Col. A.J. Biddle, Capt. W.E. Fairbairn, and former Marine Mr. John Styers for their professional acumen on blade fighting. What is often overlooked is that all these distinguished authors' teachings and training methods were carried out during wartime. They actually taught combat soldiers from a variety of countries and armies to kill the enemy with a knife or other edged weapon!

The fighting systems each favored—which were constantly updated based upon first-hand experiences or the experiences of their students—were simply the vehicles by which they imparted their knowledge to men *already prepared* to conduct brutal warfare against an identified enemy. For this reason alone, as any professional military instructor can tell us, the learning curve for combatives drops dramatically when compared to the civilian student of the martial arts.

The combat soldier's world revolves around his weapon systems. His proficiency with rifle, pistol, light machine gun, antitank rocket, and an assortment of other specialized items of military hardware ensures his survival as well as mission accomplishment. This skill, when combined with individual and unit tactics, permits the combat soldier to successfully close with the armed enemy and to defeat/destroy him.

Overall military hand-to-hand combatives programs instruct in a variety of subjects, one of which is the knife. Direct evidence of this is seen in such texts as *Cold Steel*, *Kill or Get Killed*, *Get Tough!*, and

Previous page: Michael D. Echanis was perhaps the most outspoken and accomplished advocate of knife training in the U.S. military. A hwa rang do stylist, Echanis trained only elite force personnel, including the Green Berets and Navy SEALs. (Credit: RKB)

The current military knife fighter's stance as taught by the U.S. Army's Ranger training program allows for balance, stability, and complete mobility. (Credit: MSG Max Mullen)

The live or checking hand remains mobile in the knife fighter's stance. During a confrontation, it acts as a shield as well as a flexible natural weapon. (Credit: MSG Max Mullen)

Do or Die. But the actual number of pages devoted to knife fighting by any of these four established military authorities is minimal when compared to the larger scope of each text.

The conclusion drawn is that knife combatives as addressed by war fighters during the twentieth century was considered important, but not so much so that it would be given extraordinary attention during training. When the U.S. Army's Ninth Division, First Brigade (RECONDO) commander, Col. Bernard Loeffke, instituted his brigade's martial arts program in 1977, he defined the military's long-standing perception of such training: "Competence comes in many forms; the most important skills that a soldier needs to learn are confidence and coordination, which can be achieved through the Art of Self Defense." Indeed, military combatives are clear cut in their development and application. They are meant to instill an attitude of winning over all odds, even if it means using one's bare hands and razor-sharp bayonet.

The chief instructor for Colonel Loeffke's martial arts program was Sung Woo John Downing, a

The USMC Fighting/Utility Knife, or KA-BAR, was designed based on close-combat experience gleaned from action in the Pacific Theater during World War II. In the hands of a skilled bladesman, it remains one of the most practical military fighting knives available today. (Credit: KA-BAR Knives)

As Rangers from the 2/75th Ranger Battalion observe, Chief Instructor Steven Plinck (right) demonstrates the advantages of range appreciation in a knife fight. (Credit: Author collection)

Free sparring with training knives and protective eyewear develops timing, technique, and aggressiveness in military bladesmen. Here, the author supervises such a training session with the army's Rangers. (Credit: Author collection)

Korean serving in the United States Army with a strong martial arts background. Downing was a taekwon do and hapkido stylist who had served as an assistant instructor teaching the Green Berets combat taekwon do during the Vietnam War. He was proficient in judo and oriental weaponry, including the knife/bayonet. A recon soldier in the brigade, Downing developed a course that included empty-hand offense/defense, bayonet defenses, and the use of the knife for self-defense. The premise of the Recondo fighting system was what Downing described as "one step fighting." This meant the attacker/enemy attacked the RECONDO soldier only once with his feet or hands, with the defender counterattacking instantly.

It was during my tour with the 2/1st Infantry (Recon) that I was selected by my company commander to attend a pilot program being taught by PFC Downing at Colonel Loeffke's direction. Rather than do PT in the mornings, we were excused to train exclusively in knife/bayonet combatives for an hour and a half for two weeks. Downing was an excellent instructor, and within the allotted time period our group of roughly 25 field soldiers became more than capable of making a knife kill. The intention of the program was to develop this skill within the brigade's line companies, meaning we were responsible for passing along our new-found talent to those in our squads and platoons. Even to this day, I cannot pick up an M7 bayonet without remembering those cold mornings at Fort Lewis, my left hand clenched around a fellow soldier's throat as the right poised above and slightly to the inside of his collar bone, the M7's metal scabbard gleaming dully where it sheathed the sharpened blade inside.

And then it was his turn to "kill" me.

Although effective, the course was quite narrow in its curriculum and heavily influenced by the instructor's previous training in the oriental martial arts. I wouldn't undertake combatives training again until attending the Special Forces qualification course at Fort Bragg, North Carolina, in 1980. There we found ourselves throwing each other heavily into damp sawdust, with the Gerber Mk II fighting knife replacing the M7 bayonet as the instructor's killing instrument of choice.

Military combatives programs become in and out of vogue dependent upon one factor: war. Conventional military units such as the Ninth Infantry Division shunned close combatives with the exception of its First Brigade commander and his personal interest in the martial arts. Even those units designated as being specialized or elite in nature/mission have seen subjects such as knife fighting fall by the wayside once peace has been declared. Again, the military's approach to combatives is primarily a motivation tool meant to hone the combat soldier's killing spirit. Killers during wartime are favored. During peacetime, many prefer they attend leadership courses or pick up pine cones.

Civilian martial artists who do not understand the focus and needs of military martial fighting systems are constant critics of that which they don't understand, almost always pointing their fingers at the personalities behind the systems rather than framing the issue properly. In truth, legendary figures such as Applegate and Styers only saw their efforts bear fruit during the Second World War. Only fragments of their original combatives training concepts reappeared during Korea and Vietnam. Those units that sought out such programs were essentially special operations forces, and even then, with few exceptions training consisted of the bare essentials.

In researching this book, I made it a point to pay particular attention to what the old masters such as Biddle and Fairbairn had to offer. Their methods were sound then and remain so today despite the much broader spectrum of knife arts we now have to choose from in the United States. Seasoned military

Hwa rang do teaches specific military knife philosophy and killing techniques to its students. Here a HRD master instructor in grappling range delivers a lethal strike to his downed opponent. (Credit: FK archives)

Guru Steven Plinck (left), a master instructor in silat, demonstrates the use of distance and checking hands in unarmed knife self-defense. Note how Plinck's left hand controls the upper-body lever of the author's attacking arm while the right wrist seeks to redirect the knife hand itself. (Credit: Author collection)

Having achieved control over the opponent's assault, Guru Plinck closes the gap with his attacker by stepping across his front. At the same time he folds the attacker's knife arm inward to set up a shoulder rip and throat cut. (Credit: Author collection)

Setting the joint lock in place, Plinck also positions the attacker's knife at his own throat. A powerful downward snap will dislocate the attacker's shoulder as the knife is slashed across the throat area at the same time. (Credit: Author collection)

experts knew what they had to work with and what the objectives were in training: knife combatives needed to be simple, direct in nature, and concerned only with destroying the enemy. Tradition or origin of any one technique or martial influence was irrelevant. The only decisive factor was if such techniques worked or if they didn't.

Today's military close-quarter combat courses reflect this same thought process, particularly where knife work is concerned. Although largely ignored by conventional force commanders who believe they can instill the warrior spirit by running five miles every Friday, some conventional and most special operations planners have developed modern fighting systems for training purposes.

For example, the U.S. Marine Corps relies upon FMFM 0-7, a 190-page manual introducing the "linear in-fighting neural-override engagement" (LINE) program to Marines who "must rely on their close combat skills." According to FMFM 0-7, close combat is far removed from self-defense, as such techniques are meant to "repel an attack." Close combat, Marine style, consists of those techniques which "cause permanent bodily damage to the opponent with every attack and should end with the opponent's death." LINE training moves the Marine from the intermediate distance of punching and kicking to close range, where grappling, joint manipulation, choking, gouging, and ripping techniques are involved.

Lethal insertion points and techniques are taught to elite force ground operators for the deanimation of either sentries or key enemy personnel. Note where the combat knife is carried on this Ranger instructor's battle harness for instant access and employment. (Credit: MSG Max Mullen)

Marines train at six distinct levels in LINE combatives. Level 1 addresses wristlocks and counters against chokeholds. Level 2 introduces counters against punches and kicks. Level 3 addresses unarmed defenses against the knife, with Level 4 teaching knife fighting. Level 5 examines the removal of enemy personnel, and Level 6 centers on unarmed defenses against a bayonet attack. Also included in the LINE program is training in the recognition and use of weapons of opportunity, primarily those found on the battlefield.

Knife combat is given heavy emphasis by the Marine Corps, with an excellent description of target areas for knife fighting promoted in FMFM 0-7. The Marines are the first to note that "An opponent armed with a knife is a deadly adversary." Neutralizing the knife is the primary focus of the Marine combatant, who is encouraged to do so both "swiftly and violently." Techniques for doing so when unarmed are drawn from training levels 1 and 2.

Level 4 training in knife fighting introduces techniques designed to "cause massive damage to the throat/neck area" in order to eliminate enemy personnel swiftly. Marine Corps doctrine is to plunge the knife "repeatedly into the opponent until he is destroyed." It is of interest that the only two grip formats advocated in the LINE program are the hammer and icepick grips. Both ensure powerful slashing/thrusting wounds that bring about near instant trauma and "bleed-out" of the opponent. Obviously, the Marines do not underscore the value of the battle blade in close combat.

Interestingly enough, as of May 1995 the Marine Corps has done away with the LINE philosophy in favor of one prepared by former Marine, Vietnam veteran, and accomplished combatives instructor John Kary. As seasoned as the LINE concept sounded, it was found not to reflect the reality of close combat as expected to be faced by Marines today and in the future.

In September 1992, the U.S. Army released FM 21-150, a revolutionary close-combatives manual developed by in-house personnel with strong martial arts backgrounds. Perhaps the most innovative of U.S. military doctrine on the subject, FM 21-150 defines hand-to-hand combat as an engagement between two or more persons in an empty-handed struggle or with hand-held weapons such as "knives, sticks, and rifles with bayonets." The designers of the army's new combatives program state that the fighting arts "are essential military skills." The objective of the program is to train combat soldiers faced with close-quarter or unarmed fighting situations how to survive and win when "firearms and grenades are not practical [and] hand-to-hand combat skills become vital assets."

Dick Marcinko (left), former SEAL commander and author of the best-selling *Rogue Warrior* series, met with the author at the 1994 Soldier of Fortune Convention in Las Vegas. Subjects discussed included the fighting knife and its value on the battlefield. (Credit: Author collection)

Army cadre for the new program were drawn from such elite infantry units as the Rangers as well as from the special warfare community. Where the Marine Corps LINE program is fairly generic in its approach to knife fighting, the army's attitude draws directly from the Filipino martial arts, whose very basis is grounded in blade arts.

FM 21-150 promotes the "training the trainer" concept meant to spread a subject rapidly throughout the army system. "Confidence, enthusiasm, and technical expertise are essential for success in teaching hand-to-hand combat" states the manual's second chapter. The army goes as far as to advocate that trained instructors under proper supervision may provide supplementary combatives training during off-duty hours. This in itself offers a new way of seeing that close-quarters combat (CQC) training is pursued by those most likely to face such scenarios.

Under the army's new system, angles of attack are introduced that come directly from Filipino kali/escrima/arnis. Types of knife attacks are also explained as a means of describing the capabilities of the

Using AMK rubber training knives, two Special Forces soldiers engage in free sparring exercises to develop their knife skills. The knives' edges are coated with camouflage stick so strikes can be "marked" on the combatant's bodies when hits are made. (Credit: Author collection)

instrument/weapon in trained hands. A sound system of fighting techniques is established early on that permits a natural flow into the section on knife fighting/edged weapons. The army places heavy emphasis on defense against attack, with follow-up techniques (counterattacks) seen as an extension of either self-defense or close-quarters combat.

Knife techniques are not made a priority, as "No two attacks or reactions will be the same; thus, memorizing techniques will not ensure a soldier's survival." Flow drills, again from the Filipino arts, teach instinctive reaction/action to an opponent's attack or attacks. In my own civilian training, I found this concept to be true, but only after spending far too much time trying to memorize knife sets rather than engaging in a confrontation's natural flow.

As innovative as it is, FM 21-150 actually offers a more in-depth and perhaps polished approach to knife combatives than Col. Rex Applegate's admonitions as published in *Kill or Get Killed*. What is remarkable about the new army fighting system is its strong reliance on the proven war arts of the Filipinos where bladework is the subject at hand. In addition, the army manual allows for a degree of mercy during the use of the knife, a trademark of the Filipino warrior. One can deter or control the opponent depending upon those attacks and counterattacks employed by the army-trained knife fighter. On the other hand, the Marine LINE program only offers termination of the opponent as the final objective when knifework is in motion.

The U.S. Navy's close combatives program is primarily reserved for its SEAL teams. Tasked to conduct a variety of special operations in support of assigned war fighting commanders, the SEALs have long suffered from the lack of a practical martial arts program. Recent conflicts and missions convinced SEAL commands at Coronado, California, and Little Creek, Virginia, that specialized training for their operators was necessary.

What resulted from the late 1980s onward was a succession of both civilian and in-house martial arts programs, each designed to meet the specific needs of individual commands, or Teams. Where SEALs are heavily reliant on firepower during the execution of their missions, armed close-quarters combatives were passed by in favor of empty-hand techniques meant to either stun or control individuals who may or may not be actual targets.

Knife training made its way into several programs, including that of SEAL Team Six, whose primary mission is counterterrorism. In fact, Team Six's CQC training is perhaps the most innovative, as the command does not rely upon standard navy fund sites to finance its immediate needs. With this in mind, civilian instructors such as Paul Vunak were engaged to teach mission-specific martial skills, as was former SEAL Frank Cucci, whose presence as a "shooter" on Team Six made his extensive martial arts background invaluable as a training resource.

Military combatives training includes unarmed defense against a knife/bayonet assault. As the attacker delivers a #2 angle slash, the defender assumes a fighting stance from which to launch his defense. (Credit: MSG Max Mullen)

Evading to the outside and in, the defender keeps his left arm in tight against his chest to absorb any possible cut. With a clenched right fist, he both checks the attacker's knife-wielding arm and stuns the nerve center located at the inner elbow. (Credit: MSG Max Mullen)

Using his entire body to power his final strike, the defender controls the attacker's knife hand with his left checking hand while the right fist contours up the attacker's arm after the initial strike, smashing into the throat to collapse the wind pipe. Note the foot trap the defender has executed against his opponent, fixing him in place for a vital split second as the final technique is delivered.
(Credit: MSG Max Mullen)

Today, the Naval Special Warfare Command still sees independent armed and unarmed training programs flourishing within the two Naval Special Warfare Groups. At the same time, it has officially listed its *Combat Fighting Course* (CFC—Course Number K-431-0096) at the NavSpecWar school at Coronado. According to Commander Glen King, "Navy SEAL instructors teach the combat fighting course to special operations personnel upon request."

The essence of this fighting system deals with only empty-hand "fighting lessons." The goal of CFC is to create and maintain an offensive mind-set, meaning an ability to "hit first, even though you're the second one to move." The CFC course consists of seven chapters and seventeen combat fighting lessons. There is an instructor's videotape available with the workbook that gives a brief overview of the program. Each combat fighting lesson is then demonstrated by an instructor in woodland camouflage and a primary instructor in old-pattern desert fatigues. Both are bare-footed, with the program filmed indoors.

CFC training is devoid of weapons training, to include knife combatives. I found this a definite drawback given the emphasis on bladework by the navy's sister services and the SEALs' reliance on quality bladeware per their never-ending knife trials held on the West Coast over the last five years. Thankfully, senior SEAL CQC instructors from several Teams, including Team Six, have confirmed that training in knife fighting is alive and well within their assigned commands, regardless of the CFC course outline. Parallel to the army program as promoted in FM 21-150, SEAL knife combatives are taken directly from the blade arts of Filipino kali and Indonesian silat. SEAL instructors train regularly with senior civilian instructors such as former SEAL Frank Cucci or Sifu Dan Inosanto at the Inosanto Academy in California.

Despite strong advances in military knife combatives regardless of service, individual units continue to seek out private instruction. John Kary is chief instructor for the USMC Second Battalion, Twenty-Fifth

Marines. Sifu Richard Chen instructs Charlie Company, Third Ranger Battalion. Kelly Worden is head instructor for the U.S. Air Force's Combat Control Team (CCT) in Tacoma, Washington, and Sifu Frank Cucci continues to instruct Navy SEALs on a private basis at his school in Virginia Beach, Virginia. All four men offer "real-deal, slam-and-jam" knife fighting coursework to their military students.

Finally, advanced yet simple killing techniques with a knife are just one of numerous subjects taught by the army's Survival, Evasion, Resistance, and Escape (SERE) program at Fort Bragg, North Carolina. One lesson objective is to "employ evasion movement and escape techniques against an armed and/or unarmed sentry and demonstrate the silent neutralization of that enemy."

To accomplish this, the special operations soldier must silently engage the "enemy" by making a vital insertion and performing a double neck slash with follow-on neck-breaking technique. A minimum of two arteries must be severed. SERE knife techniques rely upon either the hammer, saber, modified saber, or reverse grip. In several of the given scenarios, the operator is required to execute one technique using the hammer/reverse grip, cutting and/or slashing first the carotid artery and then the larynx. The final technique is an overhead strike, using the icepick grip to insert the knife at the juncture of the neck and shoulder so as to catch the collarbone as a guide.

Again, as with all those previous military fighting systems discussed, we see a firm foundation laid in empty-hand techniques, to include punching, kicking, grabbing, throwing, and grappling. Even so, unlike mainstream civilian martial arts instruction, the introduction of weapons is almost parallel to empty-hand fighting as promoted by the U.S. military. Long-term CQC programs are given emphasis in the realization that such skills are short term in duration unless encouraged to be maintained at high levels of readiness.

Still, the armed forces are not returning irresponsible martial arts killers to our not-so-gentle society, as some might fear. The counterbalance to such skills lies in the strong moral, ethical, and professional standards set by the military for its personnel, particularly those assigned to such combat arms specialties as infantry and armor. This mirrors the commitment to a higher plane of thinking and action promoted by most martial arts, regardless of origin.

It was with this background that I began my own evolution in knife combatives. What I brought with me was physical ability, a warrior's mind-set, and a commitment to learn something new in order to become more proficient as a practitioner.

My house, as they say, was built on solid ground.

THE KNIFE

CHAPTER TWO

"A knife fighter without a knife is a pretty sorry animal."

James Keating, COMTECH

Any knife can be a "fighting knife" regardless of whether the individual is trained or untrained in its use as such. According to the FBI, for years now the vast majority of stabbings in the United States have been committed with screwdrivers. Where actual knife assaults/defenses are at issue, it is the common kitchen knife most often taken into evidence. Clearly, the average American relies upon the average instrument at hand when it comes to what might be called "knife fighting."

Professional opinions abound on what constitutes a fighting knife over one termed as a combat or camp/utility tool. Rex Applegate, grand old man of close combatives and a true national treasure on the subject, believes a fighting knife must be double edged, razor sharp, and possessing a point sharp enough to penetrate protective layers of clothing while tough enough to withstand intense lateral pressures. On the other hand, the late Bo Randall based his legendary Randall #1 Fighting Knife on a single edge design having the same attributes as promoted by Colonel Applegate, and it is safe to say that far more #1s have seen combat than Applegate-Fairbairn fighters.

If we broaden our expert base, the ideal fighting knife defined by Filipino bladesmen is the butterfly, or balisong folder, which is normally single edged, although a variety of blade patterns are found in this category of bladeware. In Panama, the most common blade form used in confrontations is the everyday razor-sharp machete. Research into the issue reveals one truth about fighting knives: everyone has his preference according to the culture and fighting styles/systems which have evolved within said culture.

With respect to an actual confrontation where you are forced to defend yourself with the drawn blade, the best (or worst) fighting knife is whatever it is you're carrying at the time. Those who pursue knife training on a regular basis and with due respect and seriousness will normally carry a knife inclined toward the possibility of self-defense. Exceptionally strong advocates of edged combatives will gravitate toward specific designs and levels of quality meant for knife fighting and very little else. At the other end of the spectrum are those who carry just any old knife they happen to believe functional for what their everyday uses tend to be, perhaps hopeful it might serve as a reliable self-defense tool if necessary.

What has been allowed to occur is a reliance on the *kind* of knife one might select as a fighter as opposed to *what* a knife can actually *do* during a confrontation. This trend is understandable given the vast majority of knife writers who are not versed in knife combatives to any measurable degree. They are content to mimic what others professing expertise have written or said on the subject, steering away from actually studying the knife and its martial applications as a means of establishing their own thoughts, opinions, and experiences.

In short, it is an easier road to write about fighting/combat knives than to write about the physical/mental/emotional/spiritual aspects of employing such cutlery against another human being. Armchair knife fighting experts abound in today's cutlery and martial arts world, and all too often their pontifications on the subject are less than satisfactory.

Previous page: The knife may be thrust into its target from a variety of positions. Here the defender has assumed a low-gate sitting position (grappling range) and is striking into the attacker's upper-gate target zone (throat). (Credit: FC archives)

My own progress in this area greatly improved once I was educated as to the four kinds of actions one can execute with a knife. For several months I'd been taking private lessons from a very accomplished martial artist whose own ability with a blade was quite impressive. Our course of study centered around knife sets, or techniques, which taught a succession of responsive actions to take when faced with an attack. Although my practice was intense and the techniques viable in every respect, I somehow felt wooden in their execution.

Visiting with Guro Chris Clarke at the Portland Martial Arts Academy in Portland, Oregon, I discovered what the root of my problem was. Clarke, an accomplished practitioner of the Filipino arts and instructor under Sifu Dan Inosanto, evaluated my previous civilian knife training. "You have been taught technique first rather than the concept of Flow," Clarke kindly informed me, "and you don't understand how a knife can be used, so your technique is without life."

The knife can accomplish four basic kinds of wounding. These are:

Gouges

Essentially a stab with a twisting motion added upon either entry or withdrawal. The point of the knife is the primary wounding feature and can impart great internal damage to tissue and organs depending upon the intensity of the technique's execution.

Stabs/Thrusts

In a stab, the point of the knife is driven into the target area, normally at an angle of some degree. Stabs can either be deep, meant to reach and penetrate vital organs, or they can resemble nothing more than a shallow puncture. The degree of penetration is controlled by the skilled bladesman. For example, a shallow stab may serve to end a confrontation immediately by sending a message to the opponent that worse wounding may follow unless the fight ceases.

A thrust is a stab delivered against a vital target area with full power behind it. Thrusts are meant to either fully disable the opponent or to kill him. Thrusts are designed to bring a confrontation to an end but do not necessarily mean the opponent will die. A single thrust in itself may not kill. For this reason, the technique of delivering multiple thrusts into the same general target area upon making contact is taught to military personnel.

With either stabs or thrusts, the gouge can be integrated during withdrawal of the blade.

Rips

Ripping occurs when the knife is driven into a target area (as in a stab or thrust) and then pulled with great force across and out of the target area affected (much like a slash). Rips actually tear tissue, organs, and muscle apart as well as away from their moorings inside the human body. The damage caused by rips invokes tremendous blood loss, which leads to blindness and unconsciousness.

Slashes

Slashes require a razor-sharp edge on the knife in order to be fully effective. A slash, or series of slashes, is meant to cut the surface of the target area through sweeping motions of the knife-holding hand/arm. Slashes can be executed anywhere from close to long range during a confrontation.

The pommel of the knife is used to strike any part of the opponent's body as a means of stunning or killing. Here, the use of protective F.I.S.T. helmets during training allows for actual contact to be made during a pommel strike. (Credit: Author collection)

The edge of the knife should be razor sharp in order to execute effective cuts and slashes. Note the use of the checking hand during this slashing technique. (Credit: Author collection)

A variation of the slash is the pinch. Here, the defender has captured his attacker's wrist in a pinching movement. The checking hand will be used to further control the attacker's knife hand as the defender executes a hard slash to the inside of the wrist. (Credit: Author collection)

An example of a reverse grip slash where the knife's edge will be drawn inward and upward against the wrist as the checking hand pushes the opponent's wrist into the edge. (Credit: Author collection)

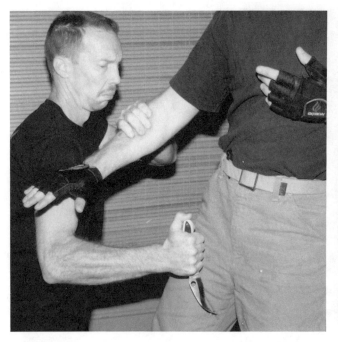

Master at Arms James Keating demonstrates an upward rip into the groin using a Spyderco Civilian folding knife. Rips tear tissue, muscle, and internal organs from their natural mooring points inside the affected target zone. (Credit: FK archives)

An excellent source of high-quality training blades in wood, aluminum, or a combination of both is Tiger Mountain Woodcrafts' Ken Koening. The author advocates Ken's work without reservation and uses his daggers constantly in training. Contact Ken at 27322 SE 154th Place, Issaquah, WA, 98027. (Credit: Author collection)

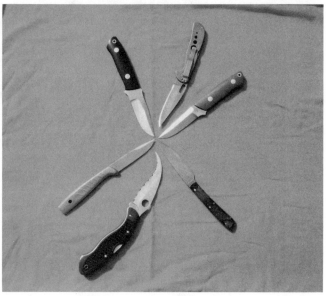

Examples of true fixed-blade fighting knives include (top to bottom) a Dozier Kali Fighter, Fisk Fighter, Draper Shikefma, and Fisk Bowie. At right are the Applegate-Fairbairn and Bauchop Witch, two of the best combat daggers made today. (Credit: Author collection)

Prime combat folders and mini fighters include (clockwise from top) Pat Crawford's clip-carried Shark, Dozier Favorite Carry, Fisk Hand Fighter, Spyderco Civilian, Murphy SWAT, and Dozier Mini-Defender. (Credit: Author collection)

Guru Steven Plinck demonstrates a forward slash using the hammer grip. (Credit: Author collection)

The rear slash using the hammer grip. (Credit: Author collection)

Inward thrust in reverse grip, insertion point the throat. (Credit: Author collection)

Inward thrust in hammer grip, insertion point the armpit. (Credit: Author collection)

A slash (or cut) can be long and deep or short and shallow, depending upon the bladesman's skill and the flow of the confrontation. Contrary to popular thought, slashes can be every bit as lethal as a thrust depending upon the target area affected. In most cases, however, the slash is meant to soften up the opponent through mental shock from being cut and physical trauma brought on by bleeding. Filipino knife philosophy offers a thought process of "three strikes and the man is down." The slash may commonly be used as the opening strike in such a scenario, with a second slash followed by a thrust completing the equation, or with a thrust inserted between two slashes.

Again, targeting is the key to effective slashes, and such slashes are only as effective as the sharpness of the knife involved.

In addition to the above four categories, the knife is also used to induce blunt trauma and to break bones through the use of striking techniques. The pommel area of the knife is the primary feature used for striking, although the flat sides of the blade serve equally as well (slapping).

Pommel strikes can be lethal or they can merely interrupt nerve and pressure points along the body for a momentary "freezing" of a muscle or muscle group. One can stun with a pommel strike or bring about unconsciousness depending upon the force of the strike and the target area affected. Blade slaps are painful and meant to insult the opponent as much as disrupt his concentration. Both can be integrated into a series of stabs, rips, gouges, and slashes to bring a confrontation to a quick end.

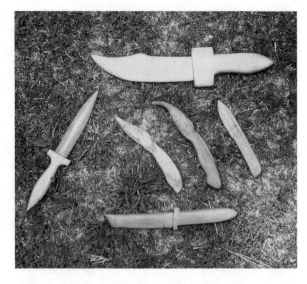

Training knives come in all shapes, sizes, and materials. This selection is from ComTech and had found great favor with the staff of *Fighting Knives* magazine. Contact the makers at 503-938-3451 for training information and equipment. (Credit: Author collection)

A fifth method of using the knife has to do with drawing the cutting edge in an upward or downward motion against the surface area of an opponent's body. Referred to in some circles as scaling, the effect is much like scraping the scales off a fish during cleaning. In knife confrontations, scaling is exceptionally painful and visually mind-numbing. Serrated blades are the most effective when employing this technique, as tissue and muscle damage is often extreme.

Once the bladesman understands what his instrument of self-defense can do, parallel concepts such as knife manipulation, footwork, and targeting come into keen focus. Otherwise we are led to believe the knife can only be effective as a stabber and slasher, which is the most basic level of knife fighting relied upon by primarily unskilled individuals.

Those trained and still training in knife self-defense most often elect to own and carry a knife (or knives) designed for the rigors of hard use and effective performance. Any knife can be used as a fighter, but some knives are better for close combatives than others. As this subject is fully addressed in *Battle Blades*, it is not necessary to spend much time on specific types and name brands. Suffice to say that as one becomes physically skilled in knife fighting and its various aspects, the selection process regarding the tool itself becomes far more refined. For the sake of example, I would offer three very impressive self-defense knives I've worked with recently: Bob Kasper's fixed-blade fighter as made by private cutler Al Polkowski, Bob Dozier's reverse tanto, and Benchmade Knives' Emerson CQC7 folder with clip carry. Both the Kasper and Dozier knives are available with Kydex carry systems, including practical belt and shoulder rigs.

The practice of the cuts and strikes discussed in this chapter must be conducted using realistic training knives. This is especially true when seeking to master knife manipulation techniques, including grip changes, and the nine basic angles of attack (to be presented later). Working with a live blade sounds very macho, but it is a respected activity reserved only for those who are skilled at the upper levels of bladesmanship. Serious injury can occur when playing with knives, especially if one does so in the early stages of knife training for self-defense.

I promote training aids from Al Mar Knives (AMK) and ComTech. The AMK rubber knives are patterned after the Applegate-Fairbairn fighting knife and make for excellent sparring tools. ComTech's hard plastic knives are replicas of actual working knives available today and are superb for disarm training as well as everyday coursework. Sifu Frank Cucci, former SEAL and full instructor under Dan Inosanto, provides an aluminum training dagger which I likewise have found to be a welcome addition to my training knife inventory.

NEVER TAKE A GUN
TO A KNIFE FIGHT?

CHAPTER THREE

"How do you know I'm not carrying a gun right now?"

A modern knife fighter

The above question was asked by a close friend during the 1994 Oregon Custom Knife Show, which we were both attending. An armchair knife fighter had offered that no matter how good my companion might be with a blade, he could take him with a handgun. My friend's above response was as accurate as it was insightful. Our well-meaning cutlery couch potato was merely echoing the much overused phrase of never bringing knives to gunfights while also assuming a knife fighter wouldn't be caught dead carrying a firearm.

Effective self-defense has always relied upon a layered web of self-defense systems. Anyone who chooses to reflect a single manner of self-protection is taking an enormous risk should that system or style prove ineffective during a confrontation. The truly modern knife fighter will be skilled in empty-hand fighting as well as firearms use, with his or her knife perhaps favored but never wholly relied upon as the end-all solution.

The gentleman in question was indeed armed and is a superb combat shooter. On the other hand, I don't believe his interrogator was armed with anything other than a brash attitude. This is a common trend with most of today's so-called "knife fighting experts" in the sense that when you meet them, they simply aren't in possession of the category or kind of blade a knife fighter leans toward. Oh, he or she may be able to offer you a Spyderco Cricket hung from their keychain or even a Swiss Army knife with its multiple blades and other gizmos. However, those who train in the art will be found carrying self-defense-oriented cutlery on an everyday basis, period.

The professional elite among these will likewise be found in possession of a handgun or will have one within arm's reach. His or her empty-hand combative skills will be effective and up to date in terms of ongoing training, with all aspects of such preparation complementing each other to form a perfect circle of effective self-defense.

It is not a question of bringing a knife to what may be a gunfight in today's all too often violent society. Rather, it is having an open mind to a variety of self-defense options and being skilled to the degree that one can access any of those available when necessary. The knife is not only man's oldest tool but it is his oldest manufactured weapon meant for self-preservation. Sometimes the fastest draw in the West is done with a knife.

Previous page: The author has more than 18 years' experience in conventional and special operations and is a fully qualified Special Forces light weapons expert. The knife is second in lethality only to the firearm and should be trained as such. (Credit: Author collection)

Kelly Worden (left) and Bill Portrey of Worden's Combative Arts are both skilled handgunners as well as talented bladesmen. (Credit: Author collection)

Sifu Bill de Thouars (left) is a master of kun tao and silat and one of the finest knife players in the country. Still, even Sifu de Thouars advised the author to "Practice with your gun . . . make your gun part of your daily existence . . . and develop a mind-set that will enable you to use that gun if ever a life-threatening situation demands." (Credit: Author collection)

Guru Steven Plinck (center) favors a balisong for his daily carry needs but is also an effective combat handgunner with a S&W 9mm pistol. (Credit: Author collection)

Hwa rang do master and tactical training expert Eric
Remmen (center) is as sure with a firearm as he is with his
always-present Clipit folder. (Credit: Author collection)

Modern knife players are as proficient
in small arms as they are in bladework.
Special Forces soldiers and U.S. Navy
SEALs train for close combatives using
a variety of weapons systems, including
the MP5 submachine gun and jungle
machete. (Credit: Author collection)

Close-combat instructors Tom Carter (left) and Frank Cucci (right) represent U.S. counterterrorist teams Delta and SEAL Team Six. Both men are as good with a knife as they are with a handgun. (Credit: TRS/Hot Shots International)

The author attended the first Delta/SEAL Training Camp for advanced instruction in both knifework and combative handgunning. How do you know I'm not carrying a gun? (Credit: TRS/Hot Shots International)

KNIFE MANIPULATIONS
AND GRIPS

CHAPTER FOUR

"It is better to use two swords rather than one when you are fighting a crowd, especially if you want to take a prisoner."

Miyamoto Mushashi, swordsman

When facing a confrontation, there are only two ways to grip a knife. Regardless of what we have been literally bombarded with in numerous texts and video training programs, the real world of knife warfare dictates that in personal combat, only the simple will succeed. Visayan knife master Sonny Umpad endorses this same philosophy on grip forms and goes further by saying that each allows for a "broad range of applications."

The Hammer or Front Grip

This form allows for superb control over the knife and is one which is difficult to wrest the knife from. To effect this grip, simply draw the knife, wrapping your fingers around the handle so they are of equal distance from the forward portion of the tang and the pommel. The thumb overlaps the index finger, and equal pressure is applied by the hand to the knife's handle.

From the hammer grip we can stab, thrust, slash, gouge, scale, and rip as well as apply pommel strikes and blade slaps. The wrist remains rigid when stabbing or thrusting but becomes flexible when executing the other techniques. The grip itself does not determine the technique nor the angle of attack to execute the technique. By being flexible, techniques of attack are accomplished by adjusting the wrist angle and that of the entire arm rather than by changing grips.

The hammer/front grip also allows for punches with knife in hand as well as elbow strikes and choking techniques. Parallel to this is our interest in maintaining possession and control over the knife during combat. If you load yourself up with 14 different grip variations and attempt all 14 in the course of a fight, more than likely the knife will be lost, dropped, or taken away from you during such antics. Keep it simple, and you will be successful.

The hammer grip allows for a greater use of distance when executing stabs, thrusts, slashes, and rolling/checking techniques. Rotating the wrist one way or the other makes it possible to use different techniques during a confrontation.

The Reverse or Back Grip

The reverse grip allows for the knife's blade to run parallel to the underside of the forearm. The primary reason for this form of grip is to permit techniques such as inside slashing, rolling, close-quarters thrusts, and checking. The reverse grip tends to hide the knife from immediate view and protect the blade from being grasped or knocked loose during a fight.

Again, rotating the wrist in one direction or another allows the angle of the blade to be adjusted to fit the technique being executed. The reverse/back grip is preferred for those ranges (distance) referred to

Previous page: Classic reverse or back grip form with single-edged knife. The edge faces outward; the knife blade is used not only as a weapon but a shield, if necessary. (Credit: Author collection)

Hammer or forward grip with thumb laid over the index finger. Because the knife has no guard, the thumb is tucked as opposed to extended forward of the ricasso. A slashed or amputated thumb during a knife fight means loss of grip . . . and knife. (Credit: FK archives)

Hammer grip with knife held to the rear, checking hand extended with forearm facing outward. Again, note the thumb position despite the fact that this particular knife has a small double guard. Sifu Joseph Bronson was one of my first instructors and is most capable with a blade. (Credit: Author collection)

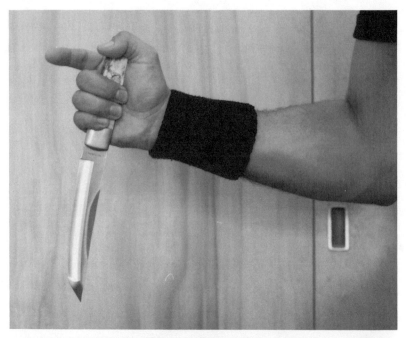

The icepick grip is nothing more than the reverse grip with the blade dropped to a 90-degree angle, point down. In this example, the thumb is positioned over the butt of the knife to improve accuracy during the downward thrust and to focus power to the point of the blade. (Credit: FK archives)

When the knife is manipulated from the standard reverse grip to the icepick form, it becomes a powerful gouging, stabbing, and slashing tool. (Credit: Author collection)

as trapping and grappling. These are extremely tight quarters where the knife must be kept maneuverable in order to be of serious use. In kicking and punching ranges, the hammer/front grip serves as the more effective grip, although the reverse grip can come into play without warning.

The reverse grip is accomplished exactly as is the front grip but with the knife's point directed rearward. Normally the thumb will once again overlap the index finger as pressure is applied to the handle. However, some techniques will allow for the thumb to ride over the pommel cap when executing a downward thrust. This slight adjustment of the thumb increases accuracy of the thrust into the target area and allows for increased downward pressure to be brought to bear as the knife penetrates said target zone.

Indeed, there are no grip variations as much as there are variations of the knife's positioning within either of these two forms. For example, with a single-edged knife, one can reverse the edge in the front grip for upward stabs or thrusts with follow-on rips. While using the back grip, the knife's edge might

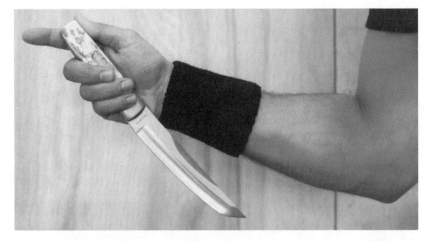

Palm grip with edge facing outward, thumb riding the pommel end of the tang, index finger extended. Again, a variation of the reverse grip. (Credit: FK archives)

Hwa rang do Master Michael de Alba demonstrates the palm grip as used to execute a slash from punching range. Master de Alba is an exceptionally talented knife instructor with several high-quality HRD video programs available to the student of knifecraft. (Credit: FK archives)

Kelly Worden demonstrates the palm grip in grappling range as he prepares to deliver a killing thrust. Worden traps the author's knife hand, pinning it between his upper ribs and inner arm. Note position of both thumb and index finger prior to the thrust. (Credit: FK archives)

Termed a false grip, the knife's edge is reversed in the hammer grip so it faces upward. It is used for effective thrusts and rips. (Credit: FK archives)

Saber grip, also used when throwing knives for sport. An upper guard, at the least, is necessary when using the saber grip as a combative form. (Credit: Author collection)

A fighting stance using the reverse grip, knife forward. The reverse grip is meant primarily for inside fighting, where it can hook, drag, stab, gouge, rip, or slash with immense power. (Credit: FK archives)

be angled outward to inhibit an opponent's ability to grab your knife hand while also serving to protect against close-quarters slashing attacks.

Two other variations of the front grip are the saber and modified saber grip. Essentially, with the saber grip the thumb rides atop the knife's handle and up against the upper guard. This form is also referred to as a fencer's grip in many knife-related texts. The modified saber grip actually turns the knife on its side, with the thumb now resting atop the handle's upturned flank. There is little to no guard present to protect the thumb or to prevent it from riding up onto the blade upon delivering a powerful stab or thrust.

The saber grip is effective only if your knife has a prudent upper guard. Otherwise the grip itself is incomplete and therefore weak. Should thrusting occur, your hand will likely ride forward onto the blade/cutting edge upon hard contact. The modified saber grip is merely a variation of knife positioning and edge direction in the front grip form.

Grip misinformation abounds, and no better example of this exists than William L. Cassidy's 1975 text *The Complete Book of Knife Fighting*. Although the book is one of my all-time favorites on the subject, I have since discovered Cassidy to have been horribly prejudiced toward specific fighting systems as well as flat wrong on other matters.

Case in point is the book's section on grips. Cassidy strongly favors what he terms as the "fence grip," although primarily because of his attachment to Rex Applegate's thoughts on the subject. Despite presenting the pros and cons of this grip, the author overlooks the fact that its original application had to do with the fencing foil, a sporting variation of the traditional saber or rapier that is not at all like the generic fighting or combat knife.

Cassidy states that the hammer grip should be "shunned by all serious knife fighters." According to the author, this is because only upward slashes and thrusts may be executed with such a grip. Anyone spending an hour with a qualified instructor in the Filipino or Indonesian knife arts working only in the front grip will realize this observation to be in gross error. Likewise, Cassidy demeans the back grip by calling it the "slash attack grip," which he offers is "a rather poor form of grip, but nonetheless effective in the hands of a determined individual."

Having enjoyed the opportunity to be introduced to the knife combatives techniques and philosophy of Korean hwa rang do, courtesy of Masters Randy Wanner, Eric Remmen, and Michael De Alba, I offer that Cassidy is dead wrong regarding the reverse grip and its combative effectiveness. According to the team of Michael Echanis and Randy Wanner, whose special tactics book series is one of the best ever published on close combatives/knife fighting, the reverse grip is to be feared.

In discussing both outside and inside attacks (range, or distance), Echanis advises the practitioner that both require different techniques of movement as well as methods of holding the knife. During inside fighting, the knife is held in the reverse grip, which "is considered the most lethal due to the power of the reverse hand-hold position." In hwa rang do, the reverse grip both conceals the knife and allows it to be used for "stabbing, slashing, and ripping." Further, when comparing the hammer grip to the reverse grip in field tests, Echanis found the latter provided for consistent power and stability during attacks, more than adequate penetration, and certainly a high degree of lethal force transmitted into the target area.

Guru Steven Plinck, a highly respected silat instructor and Special Forces soldier, once reviewed Cassidy's book in my presence and offered his opinion. "It's a good book in many areas," he told me, "but it's obviously written by knife makers who have little practical experience fighting with knives." Plinck also noted the text's lack of understanding when it came to the concept and importance of distance/range as demonstrated in the book's illustrations. "It's a very traditional European approach to knife fighting," he concluded.

And this is true. Cassidy clearly draws an enormous amount of influence from Applegate, Sykes, Biddle, and John Styers, all of who were military instructors steeped primarily in the Western sword fighting systems of long ago. Cassidy addresses the Asian arts only briefly, and then it is primarily Japanese sword philosophy he touches upon. Neither Western or Eastern sword disciplines have

An inverted hammer grip (front) being interdicted by a knife held in a saber grip (rear). The target zone of the rear knife is the "snake's" wrist holding the opposing blade. Knife advocates often wear protective leather gauntlets such as those shown to protect this vital area. (Credit: Author collection)

In grappling range, the reverse grip allows the knife to be used effectively. Here a joint manipulation has been used to control the opponent while the knife is held in such a manner to permit either a pommel strike to the temple/face or slash/thrust to the throat. (Credit: Author collection)

anything to do with knife combatives, and Japan hardly represents the length and breadth of knife-related martial practices throughout southeast and southwest Asia. Had Cassidy been aware of and studied either kali or silat, for example, his tune would have sounded far different.

This is not to say Bill Cassidy hasn't given us a valuable resource on knife combatives, because he truly has. At the same time, far too many early texts on the subject are riddled with the kinds of misconceptions, partial truths, and outright errors suffered by Cassidy's treatment of the craft. This in turn has led students of knife combatives who rely upon such texts to pursue the faults of the author as truth, and in this area such bad information can prove fatal.

Concentrate on the front and back grip forms when handling your knife. Experiment with the weapon's placement in your hand from these two grip forms. With a training knife, practice moving it from one grip to the other until it becomes second nature. Then, begin adjusting the knife in your hand to fill in the variations that translate as individual techniques of attack/defense directed by opportunity and target zone. (I strongly advocate James Keating's superlative three-volume video program *ComTech Knife Craft*. Keating presents clear and concise instruction in blade manipulation and grips, including practical exercises to develop and strengthen one's attributes in this area. He possesses a solid base in

James Keating, blademaster, demonstrates proper stance and grip when delivering the thrust. Note the use of the saber grip due to the large protective guard that allows fingers to be positioned properly. (Credit: Author collection)

As Keating executes the thrust, he drives the knife directly into the target, positioning his body to allow for maximum reach yet limiting his own target zones for a counterattack by the opponent. (Credit: Author collection)

kali as well as in the American, Mexican, and European fighting systems. The investment is minimal and well worth your training time.)

Another widely misunderstood grip form is the ice-pick grip, which is nothing more than a variation of the back or reverse grip. I believe much of today's disdain for this form is derived from a misreading of Colonel Applegate's observations in *Kill or Get Killed*. The colonel states that the grip which allows for *only* an upward or downward thrust is *probably* used by the unskilled or those who have received little "training in the use of the knife as a weapon." The author further opines that demented people commonly grasp a knife in such a fashion, as do those who use knives during crimes of passion.

Cassidy mimics Applegate's observations sans apparent question or shame. On the other hand, John Styers in *Cold Steel* shows true heart in relying upon a single grip form, that being the saber grip. As an ardent student of A.J. Biddle's combatives school, I do not find this surprising. Styers supports his grip choice by relying upon the bowie-style knife with large double guard.

What Applegate points out regarding the ice-pick as well as hammer grips is our natural inclination to grasp such a tool in these fashions. He is clear when describing unskilled or unbalanced individuals employing knives in such grips for just this reason. However, Applegate does not downplay the value of the front or back grip when used by *skilled* and clear-thinking knife fighters, even though he underrates the range of motion these grip forms truly afford.

As a variation of the reverse grip, the ice-pick grip is used properly for a total power thrusting attack which can become a devastating rip or gouge during secondary attacks to the same target zones. Or the ice-pick attack may be the secondary wounding, perhaps as a follow-on to a reverse grip slash or hammer grip thrust. This comes about through understanding the knife's capabilities and through actual training in effective knife fighting systems such as kali or hwa rang do.

The lesson I have learned from my own training is to concentrate on two primary grip forms while exploring their natural variations. Also, I question more closely information that is presently available and qualify it on the basis of personal application as well as the expertise of others representing perhaps different trains of thought. Grip forms and knife manipulations are not complicated, nor are they difficult to execute/perform. Keep it simple, practice often, and know your chosen silent partner's unique traits. From here, we can move on to the importance of footwork and the appreciation of distance.

MOBILITY AND RANGE

CHAPTER FIVE

"Mobility is the ability to quickly and smoothly move from one position to another. Range is defined by distance, not weapons. The ability to effectively use a weapon depends greatly on the spatial relationship between combatants."

Sifu Richard Chen, Combatives Instructor
3rd Bn., Co. C, 75th Ranger Regt.

Once it is understood how a knife can be used as a weapon and which grip forms are necessary to learn and utilize during training, the student of blade combatives must address the concepts of mobility and distance/range where these apply to actual fighting.

As noted earlier, Guru Steven Plinck places great emphasis on both footwork and a complete understanding of distance and its direct influence on physical confrontation. In researching various other texts related to knife fighting, I discovered most, if not all, only touched upon the issue of range in a knife fight. Most of the opinions given turned to the length of the knife's blade as a measure of distance, which is the obvious answer to those unskilled or of limited experience in the martial arts.

Distance as a priority factor in knife fighting was taught to me by Sifu Paul Vunak, a full instructor in the Filipino martial arts and director of Progressive Fighting Systems (PFS). Vunak points out that the vast majority of those techniques taught about knife fighting are unworkable and irresponsible. For example, how often do we see counterknife and empty-hand disarms pictured in books and magazine articles? "The attacker is always pictured with his knife locked out or coming down in a committed stab," says Sifu Paul. "No one fights with a knife this way, so these techniques won't work on the street. Knife fighting is fast, with the knife popping in and then being retracted. To attempt a disarm using empty-hand techniques or to use traditional karate blocks against a knife fighter is suicide!"

In fact, traditional karate training in the United States rarely teaches knife fighting, and when conventional martial arts instructors do, the coursework is most often flawed. This is because since 1970, karate/judo in America has evolved into strictly sports training, with weapons training becoming entertainment. Many "instructors" today teach that the skilled empty-hands practitioner can overcome a weapon-wielding attacker, and this is dead wrong. In truth, the vast majority of martial arts instructors haven't a clue as to knife combat, and whatever it is they teach will most likely get the trusting—and paying—student maimed or killed.

In turning to the Filipino art of kali, I found Sifu Paul's instruction on the importance of distance to be one of several critical nodes of successful knife self-defense. Kali is a blade art due to the rich historical culture of the Philippines, where the knife is central to daily living. Under constant threat of invasion from nearly every seafaring country or empire in the known world, the Filipino people developed a series of fighting systems that were both original and eclectic, depending upon whom they faced in combat at any given time. The same holds true for the Indonesian fighting arts, of which silat is the primary generic martial practice. As Sifu Bill de Thouars has said, "Without the knife there is no silat."

Previous page: Fencing demands great mobility and most often is executed at kicking range due to the length of the foils used in this blade sport. Although some techniques and concepts can be applied to knife fighting, fencing is fencing and bladework is not. (Credit: Author collection)

Kicking range is when you can deliver a kick to your opponent at full leg length plus six inches. Knife fighters most often train low gate kicks, foot sweeps, and knee destructions in this range. (Credit: MSG Max Mullen)

Blade length and type allows for greater use of the four fighting ranges. The khukuri, for example, allows for killing strikes to be delivered from long range and hence provides greater safety to the defender. (Credit: FK archives)

The author (right) believes free sparring to be the final stage in proper combative knife instruction. Note the range each fighter is in as well as grip form, position of checking hands, and highly mobile stances. Free sparring consists of 30-second bouts with no quarter asked or given. (Credit: FC archives)

The stances of both fighters display stable launch platforms possessing both balance and instant mobility. Sifu Joseph Bronson (left) relies on the modified saber grip, knife to the rear and checking hand extended at a 45-degree angle. (Credit: FC archives)

Using the saber grip, knife to the rear, Gary Griffin (left) maintains kicking range as he determines his opponent's intent and possible moves. Again, the checking hand is extended but is in a 90-degree angle. This is personal preference on the part of each fighter. Remember, in knife fighting you can violate technique but not principle. (Credit: FK archives)

Distance or range is the spatial relationship between combatants. Fighting range will vary according to those people involved. Some have long legs and short arms, others just the opposite, and still others are equally as different in their physical make-up. The range between fighters is called the "gap," and the gap must be bridged by one fighter or the other in order for effective strikes to be delivered.

The gap is bridged using a combination of individual techniques. Footwork is critical to the successful exploitation of range and must be developed parallel to actual knife fighting techniques. Combative footwork means not only being able to smoothly cover distance while striking but the ability to evade oncoming strikes coming from one's opponent.

Mobility, therefore, is the enhanced ability to utilize range to one's best advantage during a fight.

There are essentially four ranges from which the knife fighter will engage in knife self-defense. These are long (kicking) range, mid (punching) range, trapping range, and grappling range. In long and mid range, the bladesman's ability to close the gap while at the same time delivering an effective strike is as important as his ability to recover, or retreat/evade, from an opponent's attack. The further out he can launch an explosive strike from, the better off he will be in using distance to his advantage.

In knife fighting, long range is that range where your opponent cannot at full extension cut you but you can cut him. It is also where the checking hand is held in reserve. Long-range striking is accomplished by executing footwork that takes you away from the attacker's strikes while you launch an attack with your knife at his extended arm. These two techniques executed in unison maintain long distance between combatants while inflicting a wound upon the attacker. The knife fighter's intention is

Sifu Paul Vunak (left) prepares to close the gap from kicking range. "Vu" maintains his knife in a modified saber grip held low. His checking hand is extended at an angle and "floats" rather than remains rigid. The author, his own knife in a modified reverse grip with checking hand in position, is stable yet mobile. (Credit: Author collection)

From grappling range, the attacker is taken off his feet and his knife hand controlled by the defender. The position of bargain is attained with the defender's knife at the attacker's throat. Note the use of the reverse grip, as grappling range is exceptionally close quarters for weapons work. (Credit: Author collection)

to "defang the snake," or to cause the opponent to lose control or drop his weapon upon being wounded. The target zone is the hand/wrist/forearm area. As confirmed by Paul Vunak, the drills developed to teach proper footwork, body mechanics, and striking techniques are what create the skilled knife fighter, not wooden technique for its own sake.

Mid or punching range is that distance which demands the checking hand be brought into play. This is because both you and your opponent can cut each other due to the closer quarters involved. The checking hand is the hand not holding the knife. It is used to parry, sweep, redirect, or jam the opponent's knife hand while in mid-range contact. In the Filipino arts, this hand is considered the most important of the two and is often referred to as the "live" hand.

Trapping range is where combatants are close enough to grab each other. Here, the checking hand may be used to pin the opponent's knife hand to his body, and other natural weapons—such as elbows and knees—can be brought into play along with the knife. Trapping range is extremely close combat, and it is where we often see knife fighters actually clinch as the confrontation reaches its zenith.

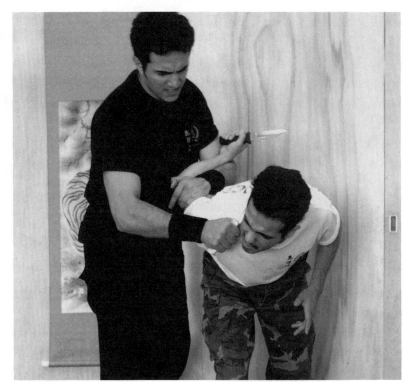

Using restraint, Master de Alba controls his opponent's knife hand utilizing a joint manipulation while placing his own knife in bargaining position at the attacker's neck. Both fighters are in trapping range. (Credit: FK archives)

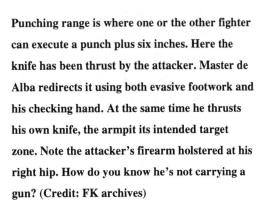

Punching range is where one or the other fighter can execute a punch plus six inches. Here the knife has been thrust by the attacker. Master de Alba redirects it using both evasive footwork and his checking hand. At the same time he thrusts his own knife, the armpit its intended target zone. Note the attacker's firearm holstered at his right hip. How do you know he's not carrying a gun? (Credit: FK archives)

Knife fighting is fluid and fast-moving in its ranges. Great mobility is necessary to be an effective fighter, as are a solid knowledge and skill base in unarmed and armed fighting skills. Shown here is kicking range as affected by an airborne attack to the upper gate target zone. Master Lee (in flight) is using double knives held in reverse grips. Whatcha gonna do now, Ranger? (Credit: FK archives)

Jeet kune do and grappler Larry Hartsell (left) and ComTech stylist James Keating (right) indulge themselves with a Filipino energy drill in trapping range. Hartsell is a full instructor under Sifu Dan Inosanto in kali and JKD. (Credit: Author collection)

Finally there is grappling range. This is close quarters at its finest, and normally at least one opponent is off his/her feet and on the ground. Knife fighting in grappling range is brutal and requires specific knowledge and skills to effect properly. Unique courses, including one taught by Eric Remmen of Northwest Safari, have been developed that teach knife use on the ground.

Knowledge, understanding, and physical training (sparring) in these four ranges are of vital importance to the modern knife fighter. Unless he can identify a given range of combat immediately, it is impossible to adjust fighting postures and techniques to meet the opponent's own strategy. Also, pure knife fighting incorporates empty-hand martial weapons as part of the overall knife fighter's arsenal. The savvy combatant will launch low-line kicks from long distance, knee destructions from mid-range, foot stomps and knee spikes from trapping range, and finally foot sweeps, chokes, and joint dislocations from grappling range. Woven like a fine silver wire through this self-defense armor will be the knife. It will flick, poke, slap, slash, and thrust at target zones opened up by parallel assaults like those mentioned. Overall, the ability to use range to proper advantage and to be mobile throughout the contest is our primary training goal.

An important aspect of knife self-defense is balance during movement. Balance means making the body a stable weapons platform when strikes are launched toward an opponent. Without balance, effective action is impossible, and without stability, critical power is lost as strikes are delivered to target zones. Each complements the other and cannot exist unless its brother is present. Sifu Richard Chen, who has trained the army's Rangers in close-quarters fighting, defines this concept for us. "Balance is the ability to maintain center of gravity, coordination, and structural integrity through all phases of mobility and stability and through any type of environment and terrain."

When knife capability, mobility, sense of range, balance, and stability during coordinated strikes are blended into one, the result is a fluid offense/defense that can be lethal in an instant. Compare such a skilled individual with one trained in prestaged technique alone, relying on static locked-out "targets" to either block or disarm . . . with no legitimate follow-up possible.

Practical knife fighting will teach body mechanics, line familiarization, timing, and reflexive action through drills that incorporate mobility, stability, and balance. The difference between traditional instruction from non-blade-centered martial arts, the average military course of instruction, and even street-level knife combatives and what we are seeking to present here is the difference between college football and the NFL. In one you play for glory and in the other you play for keeps.

Qualify potential instructors and resource materials with this chapter in mind. The total knife fighter is multitalented and option inclined. He is water and fire at the same instant, devoid of overly complicated technique and impossible to fix in any one spot. When he strikes, it is without hesitation or warning, and it is always through the target with accuracy and power. Any other approach is suicide.

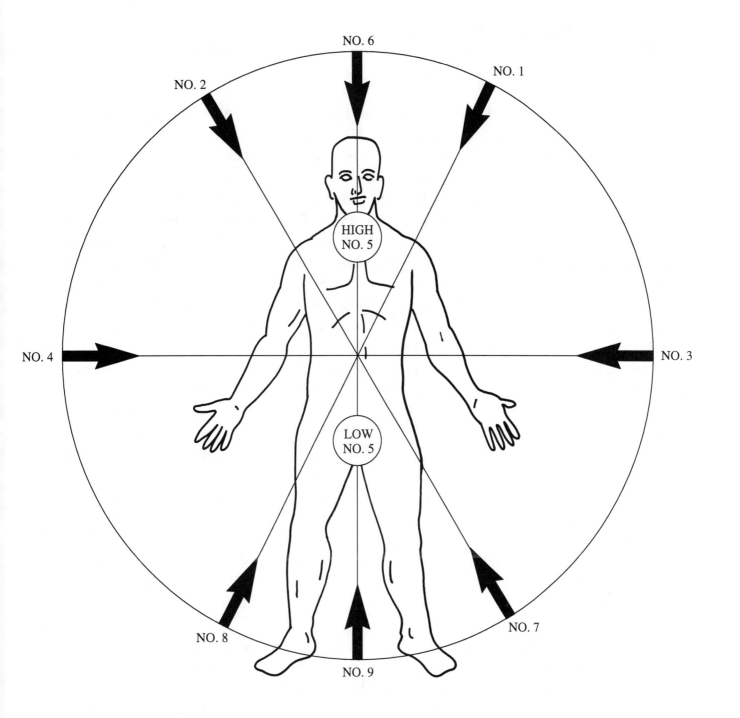

LINE FAMILIARIZATION

CHAPTER SIX

"See what you hit and hit what you see."

Special Forces sniper adage

The knife is second only to the handgun as a lethal form of self-defense. Those who downplay this truth only exhibit their ignorance on the subject and do a great disservice to those seeking a viable option to firearms carry and use. To understand just how effective the knife becomes in skilled hands, we must explore line familiarization and angles of attack.

When we possess a working, reflexive knowledge of all those possible angles of attack which the human body is vulnerable to, we possess line familiarization. Each angle of attack represents a single line for the knife to travel along toward a selected target zone. Line familiarization also teaches the knife fighter what natural weapons the body can offer and how to either neutralize these or stay out of their way. Angles of attack utilize the knife's essential capabilities to inflict wounds and demand coordinated movement to access. Universal in application, such angles remain constant regardless of the range we're fighting in, as only targets of opportunity are of interest to us.

In order to both memorize and practice these attack angles, we must establish a pattern that facilitates the learning procedure. Before doing so, I give thanks to Sifu Dan Inosanto for his wise instruction in this area, which I shall draw heavily from for the remainder of this chapter.

For the purposes of this book, we will train nine angles of attack as established within the Filipino blade systems. Bear in mind that there are numerous such fighting styles within the bounds of kali, escrima, and arnis. The nine angles presented here provide the most compact representation I believe necessary for knife self-defense.

To frame the pattern we rely upon a + sign, an x sign, and a dot (•). Knife attacks fall into these three mathematic symbols in the sense that they represent the angles at which a knife can be delivered into a selected target zone.

The + sign represents vertical and horizontal strikes, and the x sign stands for diagonal attacks. The dot (•) represents thrusts, pokes, gouges, or stabs. The knife is directed along these pathways to form either a single or series of attacks. It goes without saying that a defense must be oriented for each angle of attack.

During a confrontation, the knife must always remain in motion. The knife fighter does not execute a single attack, then stand back to see what its effect was. The knife flows in a smooth, random pattern of attacks until the confrontation is brought to a halt by either the opponent quitting or being taken to the ground. Knife offense/defense is flexible in that nothing is taken for granted. Never rely upon one technique or strike in a fight. The bladesman will train in both offense and defense, and there are no secret blocks or strikes that cannot be overcome by either skill or blind luck.

Each of our nine angles is numbered as a means of quick reference and aid during training. These are as follows:

Previous page: The nine angles of attack for any of the four strikes discussed are presented in this matrix. Angles must be defended as well as exploited, and at all three gate levels.

Number 1—Downward diagonal slash, stab, or strike toward the left side of the opponent's head, neck, torso, or lower body.

Number 2—Downward diagonal slash, stab, or strike toward the right side of the opponent's head, neck, torso, or lower body.

Number 3—Horizontal slash from the opponent's left torso area to the right. Targets may be ribs, side, belly, or hip area.

Number 4—Horizontal slash from the opponent's right torso area to the left. Targets are same as Number 3.

Number 5—Thrust, stab, or pommel strike launched directly into the opponent's front. Targets include face, chest, belly, groin, arms, and legs.

Number 6—Any attack, normally a thrust, directed in a straight downward line upon the opponent.

Number 7—Upward diagonal slash beginning normally at the opponent's lower left side of the body.

Number 8—Upward diagonal slash beginning normally at the opponent's lower right side of the body.

Number 9—Any attack, normally a thrust, directed straight up into the opponent's body.

The body is also divided horizontally into three planes, or gates. From the top of the head to the base of the neck is the upper gate. From the base of the neck to the lower belly is the middle gate. And from the lower belly line to the bottom of the feet is the lower gate. Our angles of attack can be carried out within the confines of each gate or mixed to attack all three gates in succession.

For example, the knife fighter may initiate his defensive posture by launching a Number 1 slash at the opponent's upper left arm (middle gate), flowing into a Number 4 slash across the upper right leg (lower gate), finally finishing with a Number 5 thrust into the base of the throat (upper gate). When training the nine angles of attack, we also train the three gates so as to increase our target zones as well as options during battle. Needless to say, mobility and distance appreciation suddenly become important as we begin to train these patterns.

To train in these angles, I recommend fixing the common man-size handgun target to a wall, then labeling each target zone with the appropriate angle of attack. With training knife in hand, face the target and slowly begin delivering either slashes or thrusts as if tracing them on the target's front. Bear in mind you do not want to actually touch the target but rather cut through the space between yourself and it in a fluid manner. Note which attacks position the hand with the palm up and which do so with the palm down. Practice each strike individually, then begin the series from one to nine. With practice you will find yourself mixing angles as your body mechanics are developed along with basic footwork. Now you are in flow, delivering attacks along these lines based upon how you view the confrontation developing.

Two superb videos for this segment of training are available from Master at Arms James Keating (ComTech KnifeCraft Volume 1) and Sifu Paul Vunak (Advanced Knife Fighting, Volume 6). Armed with either of these, the student will receive a visual explanation of how the angles of attack are to be trained, which, when used in conjunction with this text, offers a full view of the learning process. Bear in mind that Mr. Vunak addresses five angles of attack in his program as opposed to the nine promoted here.

Parallel to our nine angles of attack, we must incorporate vital areas of knife insertion when using the thrust. The untrained or poorly skilled knife user will stab and slash at anything offered him in the hope of seeing success. Any idiot can pick up a knife and engage in a free-for-all cutting spree. The

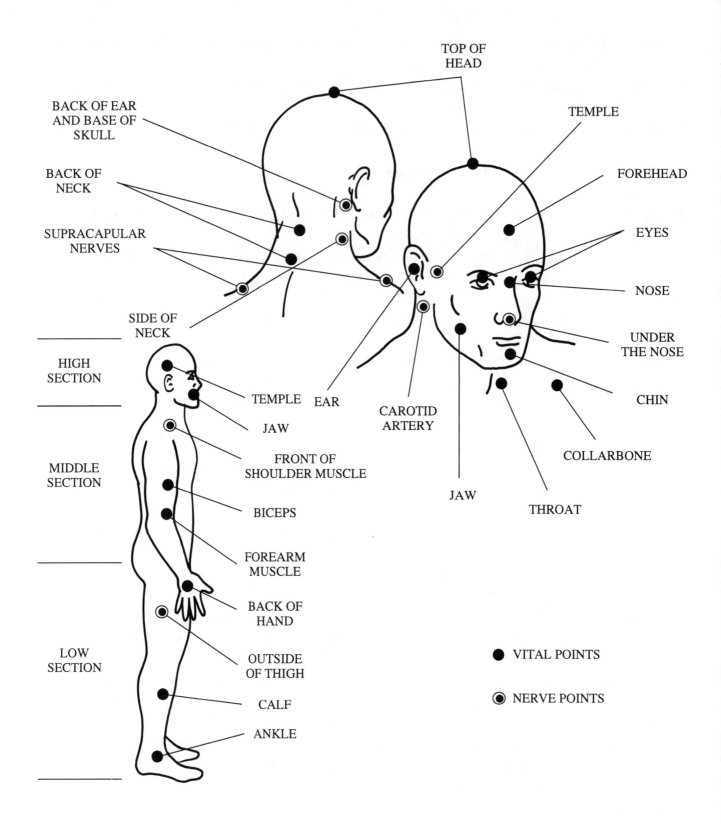

TOP OF
HEAD

TEMPLE

FOREHEAD

BACK OF EAR
AND BASE OF
SKULL

EYES

BACK OF
NECK

NOSE

SUPRACAPULAR
NERVES

UNDER
THE NOSE

SIDE OF
NECK

CHIN

HIGH
SECTION

TEMPLE   EAR

CAROTID
ARTERY

JAW

COLLARBONE

FRONT OF
SHOULDER MUSCLE

JAW   THROAT

MIDDLE
SECTION

BICEPS

FOREARM
MUSCLE

BACK OF
HAND

LOW
SECTION

OUTSIDE
OF THIGH

● VITAL POINTS

◉ NERVE POINTS

CALF

ANKLE

Vital targets for knife strikes are shown here. The knife fighter studies the human anatomy for the purpose of launching effective strikes. Insertion points include the temple, back of neck, throat, eye sockets, under the chin, and ear. Note the three gate levels—high, middle, and low.

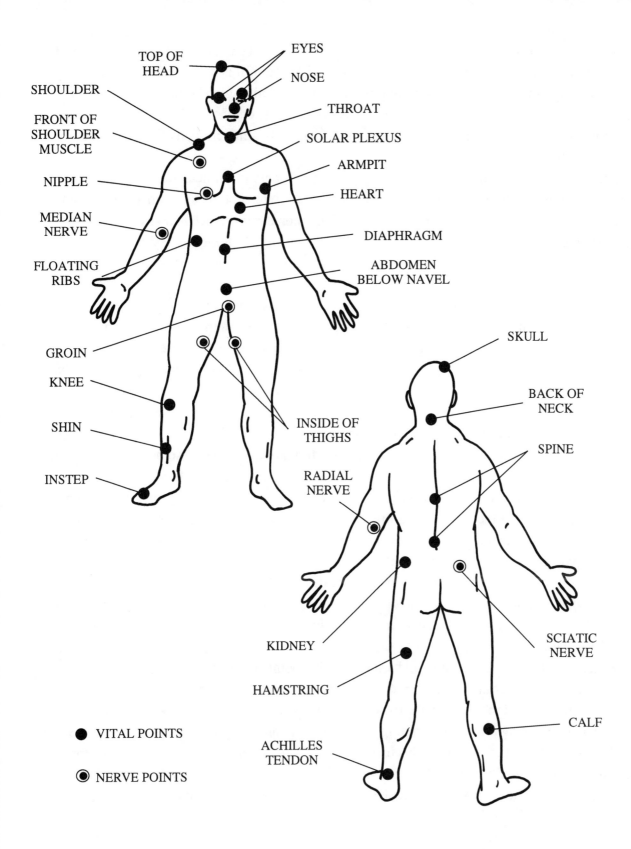

TOP OF HEAD

EYES

NOSE

SHOULDER

THROAT

FRONT OF SHOULDER MUSCLE

SOLAR PLEXUS

ARMPIT

NIPPLE

HEART

MEDIAN NERVE

DIAPHRAGM

FLOATING RIBS

ABDOMEN BELOW NAVEL

GROIN

KNEE

SHIN

INSIDE OF THIGHS

INSTEP

SKULL

BACK OF NECK

SPINE

RADIAL NERVE

SCIATIC NERVE

KIDNEY

HAMSTRING

CALF

ACHILLES TENDON

● VITAL POINTS

◉ NERVE POINTS

Vital targets in the middle and low gates include the armpit, solar plexus (heart/lungs), diaphragm, abdomen below the navel, hamstring, and Achilles' tendon. Blood pathways affected by accurate slashes and sometimes thrusts are present in the neck/throat area, along the arms and legs, and deep within the body cavity such as the stomach artery.

expert knife player studies human anatomy with the intensity of a surgeon. The right strike at the right point is his goal. A fight can be concluded with a single shallow cut if it is delivered properly.

Knife insertion points are reserved for killing blows. This is a lethal-force situation and the one most normally faced by military personnel engaged in combat operations. On the civilian side of the fence, law enforcement officers, emergency response personnel, and upstanding civilians should be equally as versed from the self-defense perspective.

An opponent gives us our targets by creating openings in his defense. If he extends his knife or weapon-holding hand, we strike it. Should he attempt a kick, we intercept his leg with a strike. If and when his defenses drop entirely, we are inclined, dependent upon circumstance and environment, to either allow for mercy or to finish the fight with lethal intent. *In knife fighting for self-defense, our intention is to cut to stop the assault being carried out against ourselves or our loved ones, not to necessarily kill the attacker.*

To quote the late Michael Echanis, "The most important factor in the use of a knife is focused attack, slashes, and stabs directed at vital areas as targets of opportunity appear in the enemy's defense." Knife insertion points where a lethal result is expected are dependent upon the force of the blow (balance/stability during the launch stage) and the length of one's blade. Many vital targets such as veins and arteries lie just below the surface of the skin and are lightly protected by bone or muscle. Others are deeper and more heavily armored. Again, a knowledge of anatomy is ever-relevant when one is delivering strikes with a knife that are meant to be effective.

Knife insertion can be the first strike delivered in a confrontation (as seen in some methods of sentry removal, for example), or it can be the final blow in a series of injurious but nonlethal strikes. Such insertions are often executed using the powerful ice-pick thrust or hammer strike/palm push delivery. In most cases, the opponent is either taken by surprise, stunned into inaction, or disabled by preliminary kicks, punches, elbow strikes, or knife-inflicted wounds so that killing knife insertions are simply an unprotested coup de grace on the part of the defender.

Examples of quick-kill knife insertion points include the temple region, eye sockets, base of neck, base of throat, heart, and stomach artery. Such points are easy to access, devoid of substantial protective armor such as bone structure, and bring about near immediate death within one to five successive insertions of the blade.

The nine angles of attack, three gates, and knife insertion points must be trained until they are second nature. This means setting aside time to physically master them as opposed to an intellectual exercise of strict memorization. Your goal is to become fluid in your footwork and knife play to the point where you are working around the training target without conscious thought. This includes, as you progress, flowing in and out of the ranges discussed while also delivering the proper strikes for these ranges. Knifecraft is just that, a craft. It demands time, effort, energy, and devotion to master. Because of this, the vast majority of bladesmen and women are the least to actually become engaged in such confrontations. Why? Because such traits nurture responsibility and a greater degree of awareness when self-defense situations arise. Truly this goes against popular thought on the subject, but then, popular thought today is most often disdainful of fact if fiction seems easier to swallow.

With this in mind, let's move on to cutting and thrusting, or better put, how to develop these skills in a practical fashion.

Training aids have evolved so that realistic sparring and safe grip/knife manipulations are possible anywhere one trains. The AMK rubber training knife is favored by the author, who uses it in seminars and courses he teaches. (Credit: AMK)

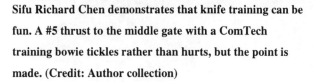

Sifu Richard Chen demonstrates that knife training can be fun. A #5 thrust to the middle gate with a ComTech training bowie tickles rather than hurts, but the point is made. (Credit: Author collection)

Knife sparring can be done in slow motion, half speed, or full speed depending upon the training equipment used and skill of the students involved. Master Michael de Alba (right) executes a #2 slash to his brother's temple area (high gate) while checking/evading the #5 thrust being delivered to his belly (middle gate). (Credit: FK archives)

Above: Angles of attack are universal to whatever weapon is employed. James Keating launches a #1 against the incoming arm of Steven Hooter. Hooter's line of attack is likewise a #1 slash. Keating, using a tomahawk, hooks/cuts his opponent's arm in an effort to "defang the snake." Note the checking hand's position as backup. (Credit: FK archives)

Top right: Kelly Worden is a master of both angles and flow. Primarily a staff advocate, Worden teaches knife from the staff as a means of creating a sound foundation for the streetwise combatant. (Credit: FK archives)

Right: The #8 angle of attack is seen here but with the sword as the cutting edge rather than a knife. The angles presented are equally as applicable to empty-hand, stick, shovel, or handy broomstick combatives training. (Credit: Author collection)

The Fairbairn-Sykes
fighting knife was and
remains an effective man
killer. Knowing how to use
it in battle asserts its
value, as it is the man
behind the blade that is
the actual weapon.
(Credit: FK archives)

MAKING THE CUT

CHAPTER SEVEN

"The key point of an effective slash is in the amount of contact made with the sharp edge of the blade. Conversely, the main point in thrusting is to have maximum power in the stabbing motion."

Master Michael De Alba
"The Hwa Rang Do Knife"

In knife combatives, it is the knife which is the power. A superbly sharpened blade whose edge is laid against flesh will part that flesh with minimum pressure applied. When thrust, the properly formed and sharpened knife will sink to its hilt with only a small amount of power behind it. The knife is as much an equalizer as a firearm in skilled hands, but its power is too often equated with the physical presence wielding it.

A number of writers have seen fit to dissect the act of cutting as if to put such a simple concept under the microscope of science. As an intellectual pastime, I'm sure such exploration is admirable, but where knife combatives is the issue, I much prefer doing as opposed to reading.

The fighting knife, or any other for that matter, will cut only as well as the quality of its honed edge. The degree to which such a cut, slash, or insertion is efficient in creating a wound channel lies with how the edge was delivered to the target. This means a proper and secure grip on the knife is in order, as is a stable base from which to launch a strike. Development of grip strength as well as overall upper body power and flexibility greatly enhances proper delivery of the edge to the target. The progressive knife fighter often devotes time to a fitness program in order to maintain these physical attributes.

The only way to develop your cutting and thrusting skills is to cut and thrust. Don't read about it, just do it. I am a strong proponent of Michael De Alba's version of a cutting tree as described in the July 1994 issue of *Fighting Knives* magazine. For solo training, the cutting tree is one of the best and least expensive training aids one can utilize (although I strongly recommend that you reread the safety advice at the beginning of this book before undertaking training of this nature). Here's how it's put together.

The cutting tree is meant to approximate the general form and resistance of a human opponent. The tree is either hung, buried, or fixed so it is upright and stable. Its purpose is to allow you to execute cuts, slashes, thrusts, rips, gouges, pommel strikes, and blade slaps within the confines of our nine established angles of attack.

To build a cutting tree, purchase several long sections of 1/2-inch to 1-inch foam rubber matting. For a core, locate either a 6-inch cardboard shipping tube between 4 to 5 inches in length, or a stout 6-inch section of fence post. Tightly wrap the foam matting around the fence post or cardboard tubing and secure it in place with duct tape. Now, either hang, bury, or fix the tree in place using the necessary adapters for whichever method is chosen.

You may now begin, slowly at first, to experiment with your cutting and/or thrusting techniques. All sorts of feedback becomes available immediately, from how well-designed your knife's handle is where retention and grip manipulation are concerned to the practical aspects of the knife's protective guard. The degree of blade drag as the edge cuts into the tree makes itself known, as does the merit of your grip on the knife as the edge contacts the foam matting.

Previous page: Failure to train balance, stability, mobility, and the angles of attack mean being unable to make the cut. Not knowing how to properly use a weapon makes the weapon useless. (Credit: MSG Max Mullen)

A strike becomes powerless as the author's opponent overextends his reach. The author can execute a #6 thrust as a counterstrike, cutting his opponent across the back of the hand or outside of the wrist with his double-edged blade. (Credit: Author collection)

Sparring allows for targets to be "cut" and angles to be played, but a cutting tree for use with one's live blade is the best manner of learning how to cut and thrust. Kelly Worden offers the Silent Fighter cutting/sparring tree, which the author uses on a daily basis for his own training. For more information, contact Worden's Combative Arts at P.O. Box 64069, Tacoma, WA, 98464. (Credit: Author collection)

Because cutting air requires little technique and gives no feedback as to where exactly the knife's edge is in relation to a target, a cutting tree exercise is often somewhat shocking the first time up at bat. Be wary of losing your knife upon the first committed slash or possibly coming into contact with the blade itself with the first forceful thrust. At the same time, make note of the depth of those cuts and penetrations, even coming from a small blade. The power of sharpened steel becomes self-evident as cutting tree training unfolds, and it is impressive!

The cutting tree also allows for footwork to be integrated into your line-familiarization training. Knife fighting is not a static affair, although some certainly train in this way. The bladesman will shoot (strike), move, and communicate with powerful, smooth, and creative effort. The cutting tree urges positive development of these attributes and attitudes because we can see progress from those wound channels inflicted upon our silent training partner. All three gates can be worked, as can limited punching, low-line kicking, head butts, knee spikes, and elbow smashes.

To repair a well-used cutting tree, one simply applies ample amounts of duct tape or replaces the foam matting once it becomes unusable. Certainly the more creative among us will customize his or her cutting tree for a particular style of fighting or category of knife, but in the long run, simple is better.

Cutting training will develop one's combative abilities to the point where confidence when faced with an actual adversary is supremely established. In addition, such training will tell you more about your carry knife than any article or advertisement could in terms of its true effectiveness as a blade worthy of your self-defense needs.

Sifu Francis Fong demonstrates a unique cutting/thrusting technique using Sifu Richard Chen as his "uke." Knife fighting is imagination first and foremost. (Credit: Author collection)

Above: The author with Sifu Dan Inosanto after a two-day combatives seminar. Inosanto was chosen by Si Gung Bruce Lee to carry on the art of jeet kune do but has likewise trained and explored numerous fighting arts, including multiple systems in kali, escrima, and arnis. He is a national treasure and a man to be honored by those who study the knife. (Credit: Author collection)

Above: Two of the finest knife instructors in the business today study the art in an open exchange of information. Sifu Paul Vunak (left) advances his thoughts on intercepting kicks as Sifu Chris Clarke provides the necessary limb. Note both instructors are using reverse grips on Applegate-Fairbairn training knives. Vunak is director of Progressive Fighting Systems, Clarke director/chief instructor of Portland Martial Arts Academy. (Credit: FK archives)

Right: Guru Steven Plinck demonstrates using the knife to gouge while controlling his opponent's knife hand. Note guru's body position and use of the elbow to stun the opponent during the knife's employment. (Credit: Author collection)

As the attacker (right) delivers a #5 thrust to the middle gate target zone, the defender executes a #1 downward hook in the reverse grip. He then rotates the knife in and up to create a deep slash at the wrist area, defanging the snake. (Credit: Author collection)

As Sifu Paul Vunak executes a #5 thrust, the author "hollows out" the target zone while passing the strike to the outside with his checking hand. At the same time, using the reverse grip in punching range, he delivers a #3 slash to Vunak's knife arm. Practice on a cutting tree or dummy is encouraged where edge positioning is a vital concern. (Credit: FK archives)

OFFENSE IN SELF-DEFENSE

CHAPTER EIGHT

"Let's take a look at your enemy's blood."

John Styers, *Cold Steel*

Society and its laws acknowledge that each individual has a right to self-defense if and when he or she is threatened with bodily harm. For civilians, however, the degree of force used in self-defense is directly related to the degree of violence being enacted against the victim. Most often, you can apply only that force necessary to extract yourself from the situation and no more.

Law enforcement officers are equally bound by specific degrees of force they can employ against aggressors. The primary difference between cops and those they swear to protect while upholding the law is control. Police officers seek to control subjects for the purpose of arrest, and their training in officer safety (self-defense) takes them one step further than you or I.

Combat soldiers trained in hand-to-hand combat have varying objectives, depending upon their service and current program of instruction. The Marine Corps, for example, focuses on a program meant only to destroy the enemy. The army's combatives goals include not only termination but, to a certain degree, control over the subject. The navy's SEAL programs (of which there are several, all approved at some level or another by SEAL commands) blend control with lethal force. Even air force units such as the Combat Control Team taught by Kelly Worden place emphasis on all levels of self-defense/offense.

In fighting, which self-defense is, the best defense is a solidly executed counterattack. To quibble about definition is an exercise best suited for around the cracker barrel, as emotion and political point of view all too often drive such discussions. Fighting for one's life or virtue is not an academic exercise when you're the one in the frying pan. When a physical confrontation is forced upon us, the terms "defense" and "offense" merge to become self-defense, or fighting back and fighting to win.

Self-defense skills are tools, and as such they are subject to how we use them. Any concept or physical item can and often is abused by the individual in today's society. Fighting skills are without form or impact unless given a physical body to train or execute them. What that body does with the skill is the individual's responsibility. Likewise, the knife is no more than a tool, and like any other tool it is subject to the same use/abuse parameter. Remember, screwdrivers are the leading cause of "knife" attacks, according to the FBI.

Anything used in self-defense becomes a proactive weapon. The critical node here is *why* it is being used. A knife as a self-defense tool is meant to damage the attacker or enemy and therefore it is an offensive weapon when pressed into defensive service. As Sifu Richard Chen says, "Defensive tactics can be used in an offensive manner and, in fact, work best when thought of this way." Chen goes on to promote that against a skilled opponent the defender must be responsive and not arbitrary in his or her actions. Responsive does not mean passive but rather that we must adapt to the situation being faced.

In short, our defensive tactics are applicable to those manners of attack/assault being used against us. These tactics and tools open up choices on how to deal with the offender. What we want is a complete

Previous page: Free sparring as advocated in the author's classes encourages an offensive spirit in the knife fighter. All ranges are experienced and all techniques put to practice. (Credit: FK archives)

operating system of self-defense that directs the proper response or counterattack to a fight situation. Our goal is to probe for weaknesses in the enemy's armor and, upon discovering them, to exploit such flaws to our best advantage.

The defensive knife is therefore an offensive weapon. When deployed in a responsive manner, it is extremely powerful and fully capable of light to lethal damage. If you elect to use your knife for self-defense, then do so with total commitment. This is where training and preparation pay off, and it is what defines a bladesman from an unskilled—and therefore unpredictable—knife waver.

Once a fight begins and a knife (or knives) are produced, the time clock starts running. Knife fights are over within 30 seconds or less in most cases, and physical injury can be something as minor as a slight cut on the back of the hand to death from multiple deep body thrusts. There is one cardinal rule in knife fighting—RESPECT THE KNIFE!

Paul Vunak demonstrates the reality of the blade as an injury producer in his video *Jeet Kune Do Concepts: Filipino Martial Arts Knife Fighting*. At one point in the program, Paul hangs a sizable roast from the ceiling and executes several Number 1 and 2 slashes using a single edge balisong folder. The wound channels evident in the meat as Vunak displays them for the camera bear cruel testament as to the knife's effectiveness. Sifu Paul provokes us to think of the roast as being our arm after it's been sliced and diced within split seconds by the trained fighter.

It is not a pretty mental picture.

Therefore, the first truth to commit to our defensive memory is that *you cannot take a cut* without suffering dire consequences. Anyone who offers this as possible—and at one time I considered such a macho action feasible myself—is an idiot who truly doesn't understand nor respect edged steel. Once you are cut, it is critical that you either step up your own counterattack or seek to open an avenue of escape immediately. Cuts and slashes to any zone of the body will produce trauma, blood loss, and a rising sense of panic which, unless controlled, will lead to a bitter end.

I invite the reader to buy a chunk of raw meat, hang it from the ceiling of the garage or in the backyard, and then execute some accurate, powerful, rapid attacks at it with whichever knife you might have on hand. (Again, reread the safety advice at the beginning of this book before undertaking training of this nature.) Now, take a ruler and measure the length and depth of individual wound channels, to include that thrust you threw in for good measure. Can we really expect to "take a cut" in order to move in for the kill? Will the body's natural desire to recoil from the source of intense pain and structural damage allow us to do anything but leap back upon first contact? The answer to both questions is a resounding NO, if you hadn't guessed such already.

If we fight in self-defense with a knife, we must train ourselves to be exceptionally mobile, extremely evasive, and concentrated upon destroying our opponent's ability to continue his attack against us by disarming him through accurate strikes to his weapon-wielding hand/arm. In the Filipino arts, this is called "defanging the snake," meaning a snake without the ability to bite is harmless.

With this in mind, we can address the knife fighter's stance and self-defense goals.

Right: Knife fighting is a close-contact sport. In trapping range, the opponent is prevented from continuing offensive action while the knife is brought to either the bargain position or applied with full commitment. (Credit: FK archives)

The author demonstrates to an army Ranger that the goal of the offense is to evade the enemy's cut while delivering a mortal blow of your own. (Credit: Author collection)

Green Beret James Webb demonstrates the knife fighter's "war face" and 100 percent commitment to coming out of a confrontation the winner. (Credit: James Webb)

Guru Steven Plinck (right) prepares to launch his offensive action upon evading his opponent's attack. Note Plinck is balanced, stable, and poised to become exceptionally mobile. His enemy, on the other hand, is just the opposite. What angle of attack would you choose to start with? (Credit: Author collection)

Combat journalist Rob Krott (left) goes on the offensive against instructor Kelly Worden (right). It is not a matter of accepting that you're going to be cut in a knife fight. Rather, it is the expectation that you're going to cut him worse than he might you. (Credit: Author collection)

In the offense the defender uses every technique available to bring the confrontation to a favorable end. Here, the author demonstrates how to break his attacker's elbow upon evading the knife. Note the position of the author's sweeping leg meant to take the enemy soldier to the ground upon the break being completed. (Credit: FK archives)

In knife fighting, offense and defense become one. "Just win, baby!" is the name of the game. (Credit: Author collection)

STANCE AND TARGETING

CHAPTER NINE

"The best fighting knife to have is whatever one you're carrying when a fight occurs."

Al Mar, former Green Beret

A self-defense situation can evolve from any physical position an individual might find himself in. It may occur while you're standing in a line for movie tickets or sitting on a train on the way home from work. It may rear its ugly head in the form of a rapist appearing next to your bed at well after midnight or with multiple attackers attempting to carjack your vehicle at a traffic light. In short, the question of stance is relative to everyday activities, whether sitting, standing, or lying down.

As Ernie Franco so clearly put it, your fighting stance will be the one you're in when your world goes to poo-poo in a handbasket. Discussion about different stances is as frivolous as the same about grip forms. Knife fighting is a fluid, fast-paced affair, with most such clashes concluded within less than 60 seconds. Because of this, we are concerned primarily with mobility, proper utilization of the four ranges of close-quarters combat, and speed as opposed to posturing or power. Parallel to these areas is targeting. We seek to evade the strike coming our way and interdicting it with one of our own, thereby disabling the opponent's ability to wield a weapon against us.

A fighter's stance is the position he takes to prepare for combat. It is the ready position from which he can attack or defend. At the same time, the ready stance influences his mental and emotional states. It tells him he's prepared for battle and locks in those fighting skills he's trained in for this moment. The knife fighter seeks any stance that keeps the knife hand in close to the body, blade pointing either forward or to the rear regardless of grip form. The checking or live hand is held in close to the chest during kicking range engagement, moving slightly forward and away from the chest as punching range is occupied. Elbows are held close to the body for protection of the ribs and lower torso, and the fighter's weight is evenly distributed on both feet to start.

By keeping his knees slightly flexed and weight evenly distributed, the knife fighter can move instantly in any direction without giving away his azimuth of travel. His weight will settle on one leg or the other as he prepares to deliver low-line kicks or knee spikes dependent upon range and strategy, or as he moves about the terrain on which he is fighting. The knife fighter's weight will always seek to become centered, regardless of the gate level fought at or from. This allows for perfect balance during delivery of strikes or in the defense. Also, immediately prior to launching a strike where stability and balance are acutely necessary for full-power delivery, the fighter will ground himself, if only for a split second.

During training, the most practical fighter's stance to practice is the military stance. The bladesman's feet are roughly shoulder width apart, the dominant foot either forward or back depending upon your personal preference. Settle the majority of your weight on the lead foot, with the rear foot absorbing perhaps 30 percent of the remaining weight in order to maintain balance.

The knife fighter stays up on the balls of his feet much like a boxer in the ring. This increases mobility by a substantial margin and ensures you won't get caught flat-footed by the opponent (if you'll pardon the pun). From this position, the combatant can move in any direction or change gate levels in an instant.

Previous page: The knife fighter will be ready to engage an opponent from whatever position he is in when a confrontation erupts. His body will naturally assume a stable, balanced position while taking the same from his opponent. (Credit: FK archives)

The chin is tucked to protect the throat, with the knife hand's shoulder rolled slightly forward to protect one side of the neck and the live hand acting as a shield for the opposite side.

The knife is held in either a forward or reverse grip, which can change in a heartbeat with a simple manipulation. The live hand can be placed upon the chest at a 45-degree angle or held in such a manner so it can be brought into play as necessary. Some schools of thought say that the knife can be covered with the live hand to hide it from view or tucked up behind the rear leg for the same reason. This is a personal variation dependent upon circumstance and as such deserves to be mentioned.

More important than stance are those attributes that emanate from the fighter's physical presence, regardless of the ready position he assumes. These are:

Kinesthetic Perception
The ability to feel your own body through its full range of motion. Applied to the opponent, it is the ability to "feel" his intentions by sense of touch or physical contact.

Rhythm/Timing
This is the body's internal cadence. Rhythm applied to the opponent becomes timing. Without one there cannot be the other, and you must develop both in order to fight effectively at any of the four ranges.

Mobility
The ability to move smoothly and swiftly from one point to another, regardless of terrain or environment. The knife fighter must have good mobility in order to bring his weapon into play.

Stability
The ability to root the body to the ground, if for only an instant. Mobility and stability are opposite sides of the same coin. For a strike to have its maximum effect, it must be launched from a stable platform. Knowing when to be mobile and when to become stable allows the knife fighter to make the best use of his weapon.

Balance
Without balance there is no mobility or stability, nor can any effective action take place. Sifu Richard Chen states that balance is the ability to maintain center of gravity, coordination, and structural integrity in all phases of mobility and stability, regardless of terrain or environment.

Explosiveness
This is the knife fighter's ability to burst into Warp Factor 10 without previous movement or a moment's hesitation. It is the ultimate surprise attack from which the opponent cannot recover until the strike or strikes have landed.

Body Mechanics
The ability to integrate the entire body's components to drive or power the knife home. The unskilled knife person does not understand nor train body mechanics and therefore does not access the concept in combat. This makes his strikes less effective. The trained knife fighter seeks just the opposite so his results are of a higher standard with far less energy expended.

Coordination

The ability to govern the different aspects of the physical body so they work as one. Or, the ability to isolate one part from the whole so as to accomplish different tasks effectively at the same instant. The goal of coordination is to develop proper muscle memory so proper response becomes automatic.

Resiliency

The ability to take a lickin' and keep on tickin'. Mental preparation to absorb pain is developed through sparring and realistic training methodology. Resiliency is different from injury in that pain can be controlled whereas an overt injury demands attention immediately.

Power

Power is the generation of high levels of force within an instant's command. Power makes the strike injurious to the target. Power is delivered through explosive action that is focused and immediate. Like power, explosive action must be trained to be both available and effective.

Accuracy

Accuracy is precision in movement, striking, decision making, or follow-up. It is an attribute that is trained in many different ways to accomplish all of the above and more.

Flexibility

The ability to perform in a wide variety of motions. If the body is reasonably flexible, it is less likely to be injured during instant changes of position or delivery of power to a target. The skilled knife fighter is always "warmed up" due to his constant attention to training on a daily basis.

Targeting

Targeting is not the series of body zones that can be affected by a knife strike. Rather, targeting is the knife fighter's ability to combine all of the previous attributes so as to take advantage of any opening in the opponent's defenses. *Any* portion of the body struck by the sharpened edge or point (properly delivered) will be damaged. Skin will be pierced, blood pathways will be severed, tissue and muscle will be mutilated and torn from their moorings. Tendons and ligaments will be rendered inoperative, with predictable results. Shock, trauma, and mental/emotional reactions will explode as the opponent realizes the damage done by both the knife and his suddenly proactive "victim." Targeting is an intuitive response to what is presented. Don't worry about what you're hitting, just hit it!

To adhere to a long list of stances is contrary to the act of physical conflict, especially knife fighting. Your stance is only a ready position that can be assumed if there is time. Once the action begins, mobility, stability, and balance take over until the final blow is delivered. Sparring develops the knife fighter's skill to shoot, move, and communicate with his weapon. If you consider stance as only a launching pad, your time in training those other more critical attributes will be well spent.

Targets are taken as they appear whenever the attacker's defense is penetrated. Remember, see what you hit and hit what you see. All power comes from the knife, which will destroy whatever its edge touches. (Credit: FK archives)

Guru Steven Plinck demonstrates the importance of balance and the need to understand angles in footwork. He has just dropped this Ranger with no more than two fingers and a slight push. (Credit: Author collection)

When mobility, stability, and balance are combined with proper targeting and delivery of the knife, no offense is successful and no defense is possible. (Credit: FK archives)

Above: Targeting is targeting regardless of weapon or empty-hand technique. Evade the attack, control the weapon/opponent, and destroy or neutralize his ability to continue. (Credit: FK archives)

Top right: Sulsa Michael Echanis demonstrates a lethal slash in the reverse grip using a Gerber Mk II fighting knife. "Warriors," Echanis tells us, "were trained to carry multiple fighting knives and throwing weapons, carrying the knives in every imaginable place." (Credit: RKB)

Right: Special Forces knife tactics include two-man takedowns of enemy personnel. Violence of action is coupled with the element of surprise to make the kill. (Credit: USASOC PAO, Ft. Bragg)

The knife in the hands of a trained and determined female is a fearsome weapon when the two combine as one. Targets of opportunity in this situation include the face, eyes, mouth, and throat. The best solution for a rapist is to make him the victim of your defense. (Credit: ComTech)

A Cold Steel Recon Scout from Lynn Thompson is used to demonstrate Green Beret sentry neutralization techniques. The throat is a lethal target area and should only be attacked when killing the attacker/enemy is the final option. (Credit: FK archives)

The free-sparring circle encourages stance experimentation and targeting accuracy. Safety goggles are necessary, as are training knives such as AMK's RTKs. Observers making up the perimeter are encouraged to block, push, or throw the fighters back into the circle should their resolve appear to be weakening. (Credit: FK archives)

DEFENSE IN SELF-DEFENSE

CHAPTER TEN

"Steel always seeks flesh."

Kelly Worden
Director, Worden's Combative Arts

Self-defense is the act of protecting yourself, or someone of value to you, in a physical manner. In knife self-defense, our emphasis is to rely upon the blade as the means of carrying out our defensive intent. Bear in mind that *any* one thing can and will be considered a weapon if used to inflict physical injury upon another human being, friendly or otherwise.

An enormous number of "knife fighting experts" appear to either forget or overlook the power of a razor-sharp edge in combat. A single cut can end a confrontation with little damage inflicted. The same cut can kill as well. Skilled users of the blade have related their knowledge of friends and enemies who have been injured for life due to knife-inflicted wounds. Hands no longer close, legs no longer run, eyes no longer see, and skin no longer remains free of scarring. The knife is a mighty weapon, and the responsibility assumed in its training and use is not to be taken lightly.

What is the knife fighter's best defense? We are already schooled in how a knife can be used to its best advantage, and those nine angles of attack have been practiced to the point where they are now a natural response for us. Our mobility is good, and our stability when launching strikes assures both accuracy and immense power delivered to the target. We are free of technique for technique's sake. Flow and frequent free-sparring are creating techniques that are effective, alive, and very much our own.

Our fighting stance is whatever position we find ourselves in when confrontation is forced, and our offense is based upon trained response and common sense. The knife will not come out unless we intend to use it, but if we do use it, our commitment to winning is unquestionable. Those attributes necessary for a solid offense have been explored and drilled until they are a part of us. The knife is an extension of both our mental, emotional, spiritual, and physical being. If forced to use it, we are dispassionate. Our intention is to stop the attack, nothing more and nothing less.

And so we come to what constitutes the defense.

To frame the issue I rely upon the work done in this area by Sifu Richard Chen and Master Sergeant Max Mullen. Both men developed a combatives program for the U.S. Army Rangers and taught elements of their program to these exceptional light infantrymen. MSG Mullen served in all three Ranger battalions, the Ranger regiment, and the Ranger training brigade, where he was the principal author of FM 21-150. Mr. Chen is a professional combatives instructor who began his training as a young boy in Hawaii. He is highly regarded among his peers and is a certified instructor in a number of fighting arts, including Jeet Kune Do Concepts.

Defensive actions and tactics are a response to your opponent's impending attack or ongoing

Previous page: Surveillance photo taken of convicts honing their assault skills while in prison. Note the center pair and "training knife" visible in Mr. Tank Top's upraised hand. In order to use the blade in defense of yourself, you must learn to use it in the offense first. *Surviving Edged Weapons* from Calibre Press is the finest video program on this subject and can be purchased from Cutlery Shoppe at 1-800-231-1272. (Credit: FK archives)

offensive actions. The most effective defensive tactics and techniques are those that represent an immediate counterattack. This is especially true when facing an opponent who is semi or fully skilled in some form of combatives, to include weapon use.

So then, what are the building blocks of an effective knife defense?

The Block

Traditional karate trains the student to block incoming punches and kicks primarily with his arms and legs. When used against the knife, such blocks are suicide, as the skilled bladesman will treat the block as a target asking to be cut. As the strike comes in and the block is thrown to meet it, the knife fighter simply retracts the blade upon contact with the blocking limb, cutting it quite nicely.

Examples of this are rife in *Kill or Get Killed* by Rex Applegate. Those knife attacks depicted are always either low-line thrusts or high-line stabs, with the knife-wielding arm always locked in either the up or out position. Presented in this manner, it would appear that the traditional forearm block, low-line kick, or wrist block is more than effective as a defense technique. Unfortunately, none of these examples will defeat or even slow down the professional knife fighter.

A block is a physical obstruction opposing the initial directional force of an oncoming strike. Blocks are thrown with the intention of fully stopping the strike before it connects with its intended target. They are followed up with counterstrikes, which are met with blocks thrown by the opponent. When a knife is involved, however, blocks become the target and lead to lethal openings in the intended defense.

The knife fighter will not block incoming strikes; he will attack them with the knife for the purpose of destroying the opponent's ability to use the same weapon twice. Rather than blocking a strike to prevent it from connecting, the knife fighter evades the strike entirely while counterattacking it as soon as it comes within range of his blade.

Evasion

Through proper footwork and the use of angles and vertical/horizontal planes of motion, the knife fighter slips out or away from his opponent's line of attack, thereby frustrating its intent. By using evasive tactics (mobility), the bladesman confuses and tires his opponent while preparing to execute his own counterattack. If enough space is available, the defender can win the battle on this basis alone.

Interception

Interception of the opponent's strike is a determined action. The knife fighter seeks the first target presented to him and strikes it upon confirmation. The goal is to "defang the snake," or to make it impossible for the attacker to continue to wield a weapon. Some refer to this as stabilization or control of the weapon, but this is primarily an empty-hand self-defense concept. With the knife, control is garnered through accurate slashes or thrusts that intercept and disable.

By damaging the opponent, we remove his ability to use the weapon, which may be another knife, a club, or a Harley-Davidson drive chain. The opponent's weapon is not something that should be seen as potentially lethal but as a target for your own advantage. Timing, accuracy, and a fearless attitude are factors you must develop in order to be successful.

Neutralization/Destruction

By launching an effective counterattack, the knife fighter seeks to bring the confrontation to an end. This only occurs when the attacker ceases his aggressive actions. This may happen as soon as the first slash cuts his weapon-wielding arm and he feels pain as well as fear. Or the attacker may not become neutral until he has been taken to the ground and all evidence of continued hostility evaporates. Destruction of the attacker's ability to continue the assault is neutralization of the attacker.

The key element in an effective defensive posture is the breaking of the attacker's balance, both mentally as well as physically. When the opponent is off balance, he is concerned only with reestablishing it as soon as possible. Once the knife fighter has taken his opponent's balance, he must not allow it to be regained. If it is, the battle begins to seesaw back and forth, and its outcome is anyone's guess.

Here are the four basic guidelines of knife self-defense:

1) Remove your body from the attacker's line of strike, thereby evading its intended effect.
2) While evading, counterattack the opponent's weapon hand/arm with the knife. Once contact has been made, follow up with additional knife strikes and include low-line kicks, foot sweeps, or live hand punches and slaps to further confuse and damage the opponent.
3) Disarm the weapon being used against you by destroying the opponent's ability to control it. In knife fighting, this is accomplished by intercepting and disabling the hand/arm upon the first "beat" of an attack.
4) Neutralize the opponent by robbing him of his will to continue his aggressive actions. Pain and injury are the primary means of sapping an attacker's energy to continue fighting, and the knife fighter seeks to inflict only enough pain and injury necessary to accomplish his goal.

Perhaps the most important factor in an effective defense is commitment on the part of the defender. Guru Steven Plinck, noted silat master and advocate of the knife in self-defense, demonstrated this to me during a training program we conducted for a platoon of army Rangers. In a free-sparring exercise, Plinck made but one small evasive action and then launched a determined, single line attack against his opponent. This approach literally blew away the opposing soldier's frail line of self-defense as Plinck's commitment to close with his enemy *and to destroy him* brought the knife to its lethal insertion point.

Upon reviewing the less than 30-second engagement, Sergeant Plinck pointed out that his commitment to winning at all costs brought him victory. Yes, there was a small mark on his forearm from where the student's training knife had "cut" him . . . but the long slash mark on the Ranger's throat from Plinck's knife confirmed the power of commitment in the defense.

The author is honored to train with blade craftsmen such as Kelly Worden (right). Knife combatives is a serious undertaking and requires many hours and not a few bumps and bruises along the way to become adept. (Credit: Author collection)

Women require credible self-defense training with and without the knife. The author's experience in training females shows them to be inclined toward the blade, even over chemical sprays and palm sticks. TRS provides excellent instructional programs, including Bob Taylor and Randy Wanner's video series. (Credit: TRS/Bob Taylor)

Sifu Francis Fong (left) demonstrates a nerve strike to the author's knife hand during a quarter-speed #5 thrust. In the defense, the unarmed man or woman must remember only one thing—when facing a weapon, you must obtain a weapon as soon as possible! (Credit: FC archives)

The most effective defense is the committed offense in response to assault. (Credit: Author collection)

TRAINING IN KNIFE
COMBATIVES

CHAPTER ELEVEN

"The actual reality of combat is simple and direct and nonclassical. Instead of being in combat, too many practitioners are idealistically doing something about combat. What they do resembles anything from acrobatics to modern dancing other than the reality of combat, which is simply fighting."

Si Gung Bruce Lee

Training is necessary to teach and sustain a high level of skill and ability in knife combative arts. Those instructors who assume this responsibility must be first and foremost experts in the areas they offer instruction in. A high proficiency in all aspects of knife fighting, including the integration of so-called empty-hand skills, is mandatory. Further, instructors must be in a state of high physical readiness. This means being both fit and alert, mentally and emotionally. Instructors must be professional in their training and ability to conduct training, to include proper supervision of a class and those demonstrations necessary to good training. Only this level of instructor can convey to and infuse his students with the confidence and enthusiasm required to produce tangible results and responsible practitioners.

When I began training again in both knife and empty-hand fighting systems two years ago, my physical state sucked. I was 15 pounds overweight, slow moving, and my wind and endurance were half what they had been during my military career. The first six months of training were brutal, but not so much that I was compelled to improve my fitness level. After I trained in ground fighting with both Rickson Gracie and Larry Hartsell, both world class grapplers and knife players, that all changed.

The experience confirmed that fitness was an attribute which couldn't be shined on. I began working out again, including rucksack marching and running. My kicking workouts further improved my endurance as well as my footwork. The speed bag brought hand-eye coordination back into focus and developed accurate striking. My weight dropped, and I began to move more efficiently in knife training and free sparring.

Best of all, my confidence returned with my improved physical ability, and my peers and instructors took note that I was serious about growing in the arts they were teaching me. When I looked closely at them, I found not a man or woman who wasn't physically attuned and committed to staying that way through self-discipline and good old-fashioned road work.

The late Al Mar, himself a former Green Beret, worked hard to maintain his own physical fitness as a master judo stylist and blooded knife fighter. His emphasis on this area was so great, he literally excused a number of cutlery writers from receiving AMK knives direct from his office because of how he felt such a formal association might reflect on his work. Mar told me several years before his passing that writers with bona fide special operations backgrounds needed to pay particular attention to their physical state. "If you were in Special Forces and you use the background as part of your writer's resumé, you should at least make an effort to honor our professional reputation by looking the part," he pointed out. "Perception is everything," Al went on to say. "How can anyone take you seriously if you talk the talk but obviously can't walk the walk?"

Previous page: Successful training as a knife fighter begins with understanding the knife as both a tool and weapon. Paladin's guide on battle blades has become a classic in this area. It belongs in every serious student's library on knife combatives. (Credit: Weyer of Toledo)

Mar, whose efforts as a cutlery designer include Gerber's Mark 1 and Mark 2 fighting knives, the SERE series of fixed blades and folders, and the only high-quality production version of the Applegate-Fairbairn fighting knife made to date, wanted only the best in their fields representing and promoting his extensive line. "They represent me," he concluded, "and you are known by those who you associate with."

The defensive knife is about training, no more and no less. An impressive number of texts on knife fighting have been written since the 1940s, most of them very brief and very shallow. I am in agreement with author/knife player John Sanchez when he writes ". . . there are many people who do not realize training is necessary to be good with a knife." To be effective and efficient at any task, we must both study and train. There are no shortcuts, no new age implants, no excuses for not putting the time in on the court. There is nothing wrong with being an intellectual knife fighter as long as you aren't called upon to prove your theories in the sparring circle or on the street.

A fight involving a knife is a deadly affair. In an actual confrontation, the trained fighter seeks to strike but three times. His first movement is a combination parry (evasion or redirection) and cut/thrust. The second movement is the checking of the opponent's knife using the live hand, thus negating for a brief instant the enemy's ability to counter. The final movement is the cut or thrust meant to end the fight. In kali, the goal of the practitioner, according to Sifu Ben Largusa, is to "discourage, not injure, and to spare life, not take it." To take life is the result of believing your own was being threatened to the point of great physical injury or extinction. The knife fighter seeks only to discourage the attack being made against him by countering in degrees. As soon as the attacker ceases his aggression, the counterattack ceases to take place.

The seriousness of knife training and the use of the blade in combat are defined by Sifu Dan Inosanto. "There is no excuse for taking a man's life, for life is precious," he says. "Any man can take a life, but no man can give back a life. Killing is then a matter between a man and his own personal conviction and conscience. It is a matter of your own personal belief of right and wrong. It is therefore important to train the mind before training the body."

Prior to his passing on, my friend and mentor Al Mar was training in kali with Sifu Chris Clarke. Mar believed in walking the walk and was an accomplished martial student/teacher, warrior, and artist. (Credit: Paul Basaraba)

This book is a student of the blade's ongoing experience in training. The art of killing with a knife is a simple one when the subject is boiled down to its most essential elements and then trained. This was my foundation in knife combatives as described in the first chapter. As the executive editor of *Fighting Knives* magazine for more than seven years, I only began actively covering knife combatives within the last three. The reason? My belief that killing techniques and the philosophy behind them were not appropriate for the majority of our readership.

When the opportunity arose to enter into a higher form of knifecraft, I responded immediately.

In doing so, I was educated to a higher order of thinking about the blade and in many cases about life itself. Self-defense using a knife is perfectly acceptable under strict parameters, but it is only possible through even stricter training of the mind and body.

How then does one go about training?

The first step is to assemble a credible reference library from which to train the mind. There are six books I have found to be of great value. They are:

- *The Martial Artist's Book of Five Rings* by Hanshi Steve Kaufman (Charles Tuttle Company).
- *Kill or Get Killed* by Col. Rex Applegate (Paladin Press).
- *Knife Fighting, Knife Throwing for Combat, and Knife Self-Defense for Combat* by Michael D. Echanis/Randy Wanner (O'Hara Publications).
- *The Filipino Martial Arts* by Dan Inosanto (Know Now Publishing).
- *Knife Fighting: A Practical Course* by Michael D. Janich (Paladin Press).
- *Slash and Thrust* by John Sanchez (Paladin Press).
- *Cold Steel* by John Styers (Paladin Press).
- *Battle Blades: A Professional's Guide to Combat and Fighting Knives* by Greg Walker (Paladin Press).

In researching this project, I found the above titles to be sound in their approach as well as written by men who have actually committed themselves to training with the blade. In the majority of cases, the

Knife training has its lighter moments. A Green Beret officer who just got drilled by his training partner lets loose of his RTK and concedes the match. (Credit: Author collection)

Datu Kelly Worden (left) and Sifu Richard Chen (right) demonstrate how to evade and check the attacking knife while fighting with double knives. Offered Sulsa Michael Echanis on technique: "Techniques are created from the imagination and are initially expressed physically through some type of physical movement." (Credit: Author collection)

authors have successfully depended upon a knife in either a confrontation or combat. I humbly include myself in this category of expertise. The student may assure him or herself of quality information and sound training advice, but I would caution against accepting any and everything said without a critical eye. Remember, the mind is the most powerful resource and weapon we possess. Don't allow anyone to think or decide for you where practical and effective knife self-defense is your goal.

The revolution in video training programs on any subject has provided us with an excellent avenue of training in blade combatives. In the past, the student was forced to accept that if a writer published a book on the subject he must be an expert. With video, we can now tell the experts from the exploiters simply by watching them. When the written word is coupled with a video presentation, our ability to actually take information in and convert it to physical action is multiplied a thousand fold.

Again, quality of instruction is what the student of the knife is seeking. Over the course of a year, I reviewed and studied an enormous amount of video instructional tapes for just this purpose. Here, then, are my recommendations for your video library:

- *The Defensive Edge* with Ernie Franco. This two-tape series is the finest such effort on knife combatives for self-defense the new or experienced student could hope to have. Franco pioneered quality video instruction in this field, and no one has come close to his overall presentation to date. Make this your first purchase and study it carefully. From here, you will be qualified to move on to the other programs listed below. Order through Cutlery Shoppe (1-800-231-1272) or Cold Steel Special Projects (805-656-5191).

The student should always remember that his knowledge and skills come from his teachers' indulgence and generosity in sharing. From left to right: Guru Floyd Holcom, Sifu Francis Fong, Sifu Richard Heckler, Sifu Richard Chen. Thank you, gentlemen. (Credit: Author collection)

Wherever you are, you can train the knife. At James Keating's Riddle of Steel training camps, students are always armed with both a training knife and a live blade. (Credit: FK archives)

- *Hwa Rang Do Knife Fighting Tactics* with Michael De Alba, P.O. Box 641286, San Francisco, CA, 94164-1286. An excellent instructional program based on HWD knife combatives as studied by Michael Echanis. De Alba is a master of his art and, having personally trained with him, I advocate his effort highly.
- *Knife Fighting Combat Techniques* with Michael D. Janich (available from Panther Productions, 1010 Calle Negocio, San Clemente, CA, 92672, or call 1-800-332-4442). Janich and former Green Beret Jim Webb offer a four-volume series on knife combatives that is information heavy. This is Filipino knife fighting in its various forms and a superb video guidebook.
- *ComTech KnifeCraft, Volumes 1-3* with James Keating (ComTech, 1-800-625-8183). Master at Arms James Keating provides a three-tape series which is both basic and advanced in its instruction. A solid effort which relies upon Filipino knife fighting skills and drills, Keating provides a sound foundation for video training. Again, personal training with Mr. Keating allows me to promote his efforts without reservation.
- *Knife Fighting Basics* with Blaise Loong. A very dynamic program that uses 3D NASA animation to support Loong's extensive knowledge and ability with a blade. Again, we see strong Filipino and silat influences in

Fighting Knives **foreign correspondent Rob Krott (left) has taken numerous fighting and combat knives to eastern Europe on behalf of the magazine for testing and training. Krott recently taught military knife combatives to special forces personnel in Estonia and Yugoslovia. (Credit: R. Krott)**

Loong's expertise base as well as a good instructional ability. Writing to WAWD Productions, 3320 E. Chapman, #294, Orange County, CA, 92669, will see it sent your way.
- *Jeet Kune Do Concepts: Knife Fighting* with Paul Vunak. Having trained with Mr. Vunak, I am in his debt where my understanding of range and its uses are important in knife combat. His video on the subject cuts cleanly through the hype and BS surrounding the subject and is most instructional. Vunak is an accomplished student and instructor in the Filipino martial arts, and it shows in this program. I would purchase this effort after studying Mr. Franco's and build from there. Panther Productions at 1010 Calle Negocio, San Clemente, CA, 92672, or 1-800-332-4442 can square you away.
- *Real Deal Slam and Jam Intensive Knife #5 and #6* with Kelly Worden. Two superlative video

Soldier of Fortune publisher and former Special Forces officer Robert K. Brown (left) is a strong promoter of the battle blade. Former editors for SOF on knife fighting include David Steele, Michael Echanis, Bill Bagwell, and author Greg Walker (center). (Credit: Author collection)

The author (second from left, back row) has trained various special operations units in knife combatives, including the Rangers, Green Berets, and SEALs. Today he is director and chief instructor for SORD 1, Incorporated, specializing in special operations research and development training. (Credit: Author collection)

The new breed of bladesmen honors the arts, their instructors, and those whom their skills may one day save. (Credit: Author collection)

programs on the subject of knife fighting and knife self-defense. Worden is one of the most highly thought of instructors in this field, and strong silat and Filipino influences abound in his teachings. Kelly is the master of flow over set technique, and this in itself is refreshing to study. In #5 we see both Mr. Keating of ComTech and Mr. Worden working out, with #6 strictly Kelly's platform. As a student of Mr. Worden's, I can attest to his expertise and sound knowledge base where the sharpened edge is concerned. You can order by calling 1-206-564-2867 or writing to P.O. Box 64069, Tacoma, WA, 98464.

- *Sentry Stalking* with Greg Walker. This video is the most in-depth look at the art and science of taking out a sentry with a knife produced to date. In addition to detailed instruction on the mechanics of killing an enemy sentry silently with a knife, it covers such little-discussed real-world topics as stalking techniques that will actually get you *to* the sentry and what to do if things go wrong before or after you get there. The last word in this highly specialized aspect of special operations tactics is available from Paladin Press, P.O. Box 1307, Boulder, CO, 80306.

"There are three golden rules followed by SEALs which apply to any form of assault or defensive situation. There must be violence of action, the element of surprise, and you must possess superior and sustained firepower. This means bringing so much martial 'firepower' to bear so quickly that your opponent is swiftly blown away." Sifu Frank Cucci, former SEAL (Credit: *Behind the Lines* magazine)

Seminar training can also be an effective way to enrich your knowledge base and skills, and a wide range of instructors ply the seminar circuit teaching various styles of knife work. The challenge for the student is in selecting which seminars he will attend regarding quality instruction for the fees paid.

Sadly, there are a number of self-professed and well-marketed knife "experts" whose seminar programs are less than satisfactory. Any seminar that primarily teaches technique or set forms right off the bat should be considered suspect. Any manner of technique can appear to be effective when it is trained slowly and in a set-piece atmosphere. Whether it will work even once when put into half to full speed motion is another thing. This can only be determined during free sparring, and the vast majority of seminars I've attended over the past two years do not indulge in such activity.

Therefore it is wise to take a notebook and pay strict attention to what's being presented so you can leave with as much intellectual information as possible to round out what you're doing privately. I also promote getting at least one new technique down pat before the seminar's end. If you do so, you'll have added something of value to your arsenal and gained an important sense of accomplishment. In many cases you'll end your training day with two or three new techniques under your belt, which is all the better.

Two blade training camps that take place every year are "Riddle of Steel" chaired by James Keating and "Water and Steel" as taught by Kelly Worden. Three-day seminars, both programs take place in an exclusive natural surrounding where all one's needs are provided for in terms of room and board. The sole purpose of both courses is knife training, and a bunch of it takes place. Reservations are necessary and encouraged given the growing popularity of each affair. If one can only afford an intensive burst of hands-on blade instruction given by truly gifted masters of the knife, either Riddle or Water is the way to go.

Training privately, or without benefit of formal instruction, is challenging at best, but it can be done. Essentially all that is needed is a training knife and a high degree of dedication. Using sound reference materials and video instruction, the student can increase his or her defensive capability in those areas this book has presented. A cutting tree adds a progressive evolution to your training program. Increasing your proficiency in this manner may not make one a master, but it will develop a far greater ability and understanding of the knife than no training at all.

Worse than no training is poor or misinformed training. Practice only makes one thing and that's habits, good or bad. Flawed knife training combined with practice of such training is irresponsible at best and outright dangerous at worst. In my own travels, I make it a point to listen closely to what potential instructors have to say about their craft. Then I watch them teach. If there is any question at all, I pass, as a poor instructor is of no value regardless of how many certificates or titles he offers behind his name.

In many cases, according to those I spoke with, traditional martial arts teachers are often the worst offenders when it comes to knife training. Again, the bulk of those martial practices being taught in America today are devoid of weapons training other than for show. Knife instruction, when offered, is primarily static in nature and shallow in content. Such training is used as a carrot to bring students into a studio, where, if they train for at least three years in empty-hand combatives, the instructor will introduce them to his or his art's "secret" knife techniques. Few students of the martial arts actually stay with any one program for longer than a year, so much knife training from these instructors remains a secret . . . which is probably in everyone's best interests.

Where quality knife combatives is available, it is important for the student to separate knife craft from knife art. If any one of us did nothing but practice and train our martial skills for eight hours a day, five days a week, we'd all be pretty impressive to watch. For the average student, the goal is to become proficient with a knife as a craft rather than an art. This means the knife-trained practitioner can execute a viable self-defense using his or her blade when called upon. Footwork is simple and direct. Techniques are fluid and based upon the flow of the fight and targets offered. The pursuit of the knife as an art form takes years of study, thousands of hours of practice and sparring, and a life-long commitment to an activity many people don't understand or care to.

I am in awe of my instructors whose ability with a blade seems almost supernatural. At the same time, I am indebted to those from this group who taught me first how to defend myself with a knife rather than how to look good with one.

The best training situation is where two training partners work together to improve their skills. In this scenario, both should agree to what the common goals are, studying the same material and reviewing the same training tapes. An hour practice session should occur at least three times a week, with knife manipulation, range appreciation, footwork, and flow each session's central themes. Avoid having set technique become the mainstay of such training; instead, use such technique merely as touch points of experimentation and confirmation. Remember, knife fighting is alive. It must be trained this way to be useful when such skill is called upon.

Partners should train slowly, as muscle memory must be conditioned properly. During my own initial training, Sifu Joseph Bronson admonished me time and again that "speed comes with slow training." What he meant was as you establish patterns of movement that become unbidden responses to those situations presented you, the swiftness with which you respond properly increases naturally.

Training teams must also see their sessions together as give and take. One partner gives the proper motion or technique so the other can practice his response properly. Training is not competition, and when it becomes such, no one improves to any degree. Knife training requires cooperation between partners because the goal is necessarily deadly in effect. Work together to improve your skills and watch how quickly the learning curve shrinks.

Best of all, knife training can be conducted alone and within very small confines. It is a martial skill that requires much devotion, and as such the pursuit of excellence at whatever level the student chooses can be peaceful and productive. The knife's power and the student's skill in using this power teaches great respect for life and tolerance for those around us. In knowing what he can do, the bladesman often ignores those provocations that drive lesser men to foolish action. With this in mind, it is equally as important to study one's social responsibility as a warrior, to include developing emotionally, mentally, and spiritually.

If there is but one rule in knife training it is this. The knowledge and ability to execute a single technique properly is far more valuable than knowing 100 techniques but being unable to use them when called upon. Train properly, safely, and with good intention. By doing so the knife maintains your respect and will only be used for the most worthy of reasons.

In training we should seek maximum efficiency with minimum effort. Training in knife combatives should be streamlined without compromising content, efficiency, or safety. Cooperation between instructor and students, students and training partners, must be stressed so that technical mastery is attained. Petty aggression due to bruised or overly tuned egos must be eliminated in training. Positive aggression and power are to be encouraged. Reinforce good learning and motivate better training without degrading the student or the student degrading his peer. Proper training and safety aids must be present and used to ensure that learning can take place without unnecessary injury. If you are injured you cannot train. Finally, in good training we seek to better ourselves and our fellow students. No one is so good he cannot learn more, and no style or system is superior to any other.

I train with the knife and in other martial skills for the enjoyment of doing so and because it has been my way of life for more than 20 years now. Today, my intent in such training is a more complete knowledge of self-defense and its applications. The knife allows me to discover these things, as it is at the core of the subject. If you can work the knife, you can execute with variation all other fighting techniques, whether they be empty-hand or weapon oriented. The reverse is not true.

Master cutler Gil Hibben trained under the brilliant direction of the late Ed Parker. When he received his first-degree black belt from Parker, Hibben had developed kenpo karate's knife form and designed and built the kenpo knife as part of his black belt thesis. Mr. Parker approved both and indeed commissioned these efforts of Gil.

The Hibben knife fighting system is based on 10 sets. These incorporate movements taken from kenpo—which includes aspects taken from escrima and judo—and modified attributes from both fencing and saber fighting. I have witnessed some of these sets and been educated by Gil in his program and agree it is both combat effective and terribly brutal, even for a knife combative system.

"Mr. Parker and myself were very concerned, very careful who we allowed to be trained in kenpo knife," Hibben told me in 1994. "The training is not difficult, but the knowledge and skill is something to be guarded. You must be responsible. After all, we train for a purpose in kenpo and that is self-defense."

AN EDUCATED CHOICE

CHAPTER TWELVE

"What it boils down to is what one learns to handle."

Al Mar, former Green Beret

Every one who elects to rely upon a knife for possible self-defense will decide which knife is best for the money available to pay for it. Today's market is full of affordable knives if the knife fighter takes the time to research and choose carefully. The advocate of knife self-defense has different needs in terms of his knife. It will be called upon to perform a specific task, self-defense, as well as daily cutting chores of a more peaceful nature. What might be an excellent utility knife may not be a practical fighter in a face-to-face confrontation.

Some players may elect to go with inexpensive throwaway knives, of which there are numerous examples. Use it and lose it, who cares? Better yet, for $50 you've replaced it. The knife fighter plans for the unique role his knife must play in self-defense, and no one knife can possible meet this requirement. Systems and styles of knife combatives favor different patterns of knives, and certainly the law provides a strict parameter as well. Where one man swears by a tanto-style knife, his training partner may believe no finer fighter is available than the custom balisong sporting a kris blade.

Each knife adept has his (or her) own tastes, likes, dislikes—and certainly his own "feel" of what will work for him. The most important aspect of blade selection is to study and qualify those knives available and how such blades might fit into your chosen style of knife fighting. In this way you will make the choice best suited to serve you well when the time comes to "walk the walk."

The trained bladesman understands it is not how much or what you own but what you know about your knife and how it works that is important. A $350 fighter is useless unless its owner can make it come alive under pressure. Those with little money will depend upon what they can afford or barter for. Something is better than nothing when you need it, and here the trick is to turn that "something" into as fearsome a tool as possible. An old M7 bayonet, with quality time spent honing a razor-sharp edge on it, is every bit as effective in the hands of a skilled knife fighter as is an expensive custom bowie from any number of makers.

One picks his tool well, learns how to use it properly and with great effect, and depends upon it no matter where he is or what he's doing. Simple works in combat. Keep your knife simple, your training simple, and your attitude healthy when bladework is at hand.

As the editor of *Fighting Knives* magazine and as a consultant, I am often asked to comment on those blades I like. This has become more and more difficult over the years, as my profession allows me to work with a wide spectrum of cutlery, both custom and production. My appreciation for edged perfection has grown because of this, and favoring one pattern or style over another seems irrelevant. Once my training in modern knife combatives began, my taste in defensive cutlery experienced a rapid evolution. Because of this, I believe it important to offer a few of my most recent observations on bladeware choice, if only as a means of guidance should the reader be interested.

Perhaps the safest and most effective folding knife for self-defense is the Filipino butterfly knife, or

Previous page: Skilled students of the blade may indulge in live blade training under controlled conditions. For the majority of bladesmen, training knives are more than sufficient. (Credit: FK archives)

The Kasper Fighter is greatly favored by both the author and James Keating. To order, contact Al Polkowski at 8 Cathy Ct., Chester, NJ, 07930. Mr. Keating is available for seminar instruction or training aids by writing 603 Dahlia St., Milton-Freewater, OR, 97862. (Credit: FK archives)

balisong. It is a combat-proven design around which the most deadly knife fighting art and subsystems were developed. As it is a utility edge, the number of blade patterns to be chosen from are limited only by imagination and need. As a fighter, the balisong can be opened swiftly with one hand and fully secured so that self-injury through accidental closure is not possible.

Much practice must attend ownership and carry of the butterfly knife or it simply becomes nothing more than an odd-looking pocket knife. Practice in opening, locking, and closing is required. It is necessary to practice drawing while always knowing where the cutting edge is facing. Practice in the many techniques available to the balisong as both a hand load and fighting knife is an absolute. First and foremost, choosing a quality butterfly knife and carry system is a must.

My first practice "bali" came from Sifu Chris Clarke, and his source was Benchmade Knives/BaliSong, a custom quality cutlery production firm in northern Oregon. A working knife with its edge severely dulled, this trainer allowed me to learn safely the many techniques noted previously. Although there are ways to geld your live butterfly knife's blade for training purposes, I recommend investing in a trainer such as mine. To do so, simply contact Benchmade Knives at 503-655-6004 and place an order.

Any live BaliSong from Benchmade Knives is an excellent cutlery choice in terms of quality design, construction, and price range. I often carry one of Les De Asis' butterfly knives, and it was De Asis who first sent me such a knife to evaluate when I was with Special Forces in Central America. Carry systems of either leather or black nylon are available, dependent upon your preference for storage and/or drawing.

Ronald Miller of Largo, Florida, handcrafts exceptional butterfly knives that are both lightweight and extremely sharp. I enjoy carrying a Miller balisong and appreciate its swiftness in the hand. There is no preference between a Benchmade BaliSong or Miller's examples of this combat folder other than what suits my fancy on any particular day.

In a fixed blade I find great favor with Bob Kasper's design as executed by private cutler Al Polkowski. This is a straightforward pattern available in several compact blade lengths and carried in a

Al Mar set the example for modern warrior training and philosophy. His knives (inset) are prime examples of form and function where the professional knife fighter's cutlery interests lie. (Credit: FK archives)

Former Marine Ken Onion handcrafts this exceptional 21st Century tanto fighter. The author is very keen on Onion's work and advocates it highly. To order, contact Ken at 91-990 Oaniani St., Kapolei, HI, 96707. (Credit: Weyer of Toledo)

Col. Rex Applegate (Ret.) has long advised the author on combatives and knife employment. The OSS veteran offers the most concise line of custom-made combat knives available today. To order, contact William Harsey at 82710 N. Howe Lane, Creswell, OR, 97426. (Credit: Author collection)

Dave Murphy (left) and his father made Murphy Combat Knives legendary during World War II. Still available and made by Dave the old-fashioned way, the author is proud to rely on Murphy for unique insights into battle bladeware. To order a Murphy fighter, write P.O. Box 256, Gresham, OR, 97030. (Credit: Author collection)

Blade Rigger offers unique working knives and carry systems such as this Dual Kwaiken. James Pioreck (P.O. Box 5032, Missoula, MT, 59806) also makes a custom fighter codesigned with the author and available with two carry rigs. (Credit: FK archives)

Blade-Tech owner Tim Wegner has long crafted custom Kydex carry systems for the author and many special operations personnel. He is the leader in the field and responsible for the design and manufacture of the 21st Century KA-BAR sheath system. To order, write 8818 158th St. E., Puyallup, WA, 98373. (Credit: FK archives)

variety of Kydex sheath systems. Kasper's knife is the only such blade I've found to date whose shoulder carry rig is secure, quick to the draw, and comfortable to both adjust and wear on a daily basis. There are other such satisfactory rigs, but the Kasper/Polkowski design is superior.

I have experienced great service from cutler Bud Nealy's knives, which are parallel in quality to the Kasper fighter. My assortment of Nealy self-defense knives includes multiple-position Kydex carry systems and several different blade patterns. These are well made, very slim, light but exceptionally strong, and swift to the draw yet secure during carry. Bud's knives are likewise very handsome, proving both form and function are possible when you have your stuff together as a designer/maker.

Dagger-wise, I am keen on the Witch, a combat-proven design made by Peter Bauchop and his son in South Africa. My own is sheathed in Kydex thanks to custom scabbard designer Tim Wegner. Lately I've taken a strong liking to Colonel Applegate's boot knife variation of the Applegate-Fairbairn fighting knife. Handcrafted by private cutler William Harsey and sheathed in Kydex by the same talented maker, the mini Applegate is superior to most boot knife daggers in every respect.

Like Jim Keating, I am also very much in favor of the Gryphon M10 from Cutlery Shoppe. My original M10 has seen service with an East Coast Navy SEAL for nearly two years now, with all reports stating his combat-experienced satisfaction. Keating, an avid promoter of the M10, offers a training video for this well-designed defensive piece through Paladin Press (*Reverse-Grip Knife Fighting*). Much

Left: Maker Bud Nealy offers his multiconcealment system of fighters and combat blades in different blade patterns and manners of carry. These are among the best available to the skilled practitioner. To order, write 822 Thomas St., Stroudsburg, PA, 18360. (Credit: Weyer of Toledo)

Right: Randall Made Knives provides the superlative Guardian boot knife for urban or military carry. One's cutlery equipment should reflect the highest levels of design and craftsmanship possible. To order, write Gary Randall at P.O. Box 1988, Orlando, FL, 32802. (Credit: Weyer of Toledo)

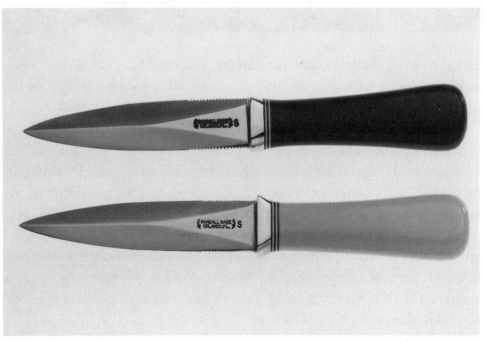

Right: ComTech's James Keating is always quick to correct his students' errors. When seeking training in knife combatives, always search out the proven experts as opposed to the unproven exploiters. Hey, he only slapped me around a little before I caught on! (Credit: Author collection)

Below: The author's sincere respect and appreciation is extended to (left to right) Sifu Richard Chen, Capt. Rob Krott, Datu Kelly Worden, and, at far right, Master at Arms James Keating. They have been a great team as well as good friends and loyal comrades-in-arms. (Credit: Author collection)

easier to obtain and less expensive than the Witch, the M10 Gryphon is a go-anywhere, do-anything example of superior edged steel. It is available with a Kydex scabbard for inside-the-pants carry from Sheathtech, a Cutlery Shoppe exclusive service.

Combat knives are meant for close-quarters fighting and utility purposes as commonly encountered by military personnel the world over. I continue to favor my Randall #14 as the finest all-around combat knife one could hope to own, but this is strictly personal prejudice on my part. Parallel in value to me is my Ed Parker, or Kenpo fighting knife, made especially for me and given as a gift in the Kenpo Brotherhood by Gil Hibben. This is a specialty knife in every respect, and Gil honored me greatly with it.

For everyday use and carry, the KA-BAR Fighting Utility Knife is a solid design that is combat proven as a man-killer of the first order. Easy to locate, inexpensive, and straightforward in design, the KA-BAR remains a preferred self-defense blade for many. In my own case, the company provided several dulled KA-BARs for training purposes during our co-development of the twenty-first century KA-BAR, due out by the end of 1995.

Who says I'm not carrying a gun . . . and a knife? (Credit: Author collection)

It would be remiss of me to ignore the advances in automatic openers (switchblades) where the combative knife is at issue. My "button knife" of choice as a self-defense piece comes from Anthony Marfione at Microtech in Vero Beach, Florida. Tony designs and builds specialty items for various special ops units, to include his HALO blade delivery system. A true stiletto opener, the HALO's unique blade is actually ejected from the forward portion of the knife's integral handle and locked into position. The blade is retracted, or loaded, using a system similar to the cocking mechanism of an M16 battle rifle. The HALO represents a milestone in spring knife technology, and I'm professionally impressed with mine. It is carried in a Dozier-built Kydex universal attachment system or a modified AMK Eagle leather sheath with the closure flap removed.

Again, there are literally hundreds of superlative blades available other than those discussed here. These happen to be my own preferred carry knives, some with a long history at my side and others that have only just captured my attention. Blade choice is an individual affair, blade training an individual responsibility.

This area was discussed in great range and depth in my first book, *Battle Blades*. The area of knife performance was analyzed from the aspect of many years both carrying and using knives under a variety of circumstances and situations. The one great truth either missed or overlooked by many cutlery commentators has to do with the generally high quality seen in many knives today. So-called knife testing as promoted in the majority of cutlery periodicals would appear to confirm the previous statement. Nowhere do we see a truly critical review/evaluation appear in issue after issue, and, in fact, rarely do such writers even point out a serious blemish.

Knife selection today is based not upon expected performance of the tool to the degree it is what the potential user can afford and accept for his money. How many times a rope of any sort can be cut is irrelevant to the educated combat knife user. In his case, more attention is going to be paid to how the knife feels and moves in his hands during grip changes and manipulation. Is the knife more inclined toward accurate thrusting, or is it a slasher in design? Can it be carried and, more importantly, drawn with relative ease and swiftness? It is simple in blade format with respect to offering clean cuts and thrusts, or will it hang up due to unnecessary bells and whistles? Is it sharp enough for government work to begin with, and can its edge be further improved with some tender loving care?

A perfect example of an inexpensive fighting knife which, in the hands of a skilled knife fighter, would be pure deadly is the Glock combat knife. A no more simple design and level of manufacture exists than the Glock blade. Yet, in its simplicity in both blade and sheath, it is lean, mean, sharp (and easy to make much sharper), sure during manipulation, and lethal in both the slash and thrust. Its sheath is sound and so secure it draws complaints unless you're wise to the ways of the field.

For less than $50 you can own the one knife the U.S. Navy's counterterrorist unit SEAL Team Six prefers over any other. Form and function, pure and simple.

KNIFE SELF-DEFENSE AND THE MODERN WARRIOR ETHIC

CHAPTER THIRTEEN

"To be the protector doesn't mean intervention is all physical strength."

Sensei Richard Heckler, Ph.D.

Knife fighting is a warrior art. It is a skill meant for use in war and conflict, and there are no other reasons for studying it other than self-defense. Throughout this book I've referred to emotional, mental, and spiritual development as well as physical when considering quality knife training. Such attention is necessary to maintain the critical balance between a destructive form of action and the moral/ethical counterweights that govern it within the bounds of social responsibility.

The vast majority of today's traditional martial arts schools do not offer much more than a surgeon general's warning about the arts being taught for good rather than evil. The physical aspect of the arts, to include weapons training if it is available, is what sells and is the easiest to pass along. In knife training, a warrior ethic must be taught with as much emphasis as the use of the instrument or such training is nothing short of irresponsible.

In a nutshell, if the skills and information learned are misused by the practitioner, then punishment by the society should be expected. Not all people are warriors or even inclined to be. But a warrior art such as blade combatives demands a warrior mind-set and warrior "rules of the road."

If self-defense is required, the warrior allows his actions when confronted to speak for him. Those skilled with a knife do not strut around the town square with "Old Bloody" hanging out in plain view. The warrior's role in society is to protect life and social order by placing himself between that which would endanger both. As warrior-sage Richard Heckler has taught me, ". . . the warrior does not invent an enemy . . . he preserves and protects but does not conquer, dominate, or subjugate. Only the enemy will have to fear a warrior's skills."

The knife fighter will always seek to determine the battlefield upon which he must fight. For this reason his training is focused and ongoing so that he can see a confrontation for what it is and make the correct decisions. In addition, the warrior attitude is hammered and honed to a high state of clear thinking through diligent study of the craft.

The warrior whose intent goes beyond the comforts of the armchair conducts his affairs in a natural constant state of awareness and correct action. In more than one book on knife fighting, I've read of color-coded levels of "readiness" which the bladesman should cultivate. This is another example of technique being superimposed over flow, and although it sounds good to the unaware, it is both stupid and wasteful of time and energy. Such a code system implies being on the defensive at least two-thirds of one's waking day, and being on the defensive to this degree develops a weak resolve when proactive action is demanded of the warrior.

By proper and constant training and teaching of the spirit, the warrior becomes natural in his entire being. He is always aware without being aware. He avoids dangerous situations by not avoiding them.

Previous page: Native American and highly decorated World War II Moccasin Ranger Skeeter Vaughan displayed the warrior's heart throughout his career. During the Battle of the Bulge, he killed a German soldier with a thrown bayonet from more than 87 feet away, the longest recorded such action in the history books. (Credit: Author collection)

Top left: Graciella Casillas represents the height of warriorhood in both training and proven capability. She is a valued friend and consultant to the author. (Credit: FC archives)

Above: Sensei Don Smith pioneered knife fighting within the kenpo karate system and is a strong advocate of combat handgunning for his brown and black belt students/instructors. He, too, represents free thinking and the creative spirit necessary in the warrior. (Credit: Don Smith)

Left: My friend Rickson Gracie has won more than 460 professional fights as a free form fighter. His wisdom in the arts is unquestioned, as is his ability with a SIG 220. Still, he is one of the most humble warriors I've met. (Credit: FC archives)

He is prepared to move without moving, and his resolve is total and without hesitation when it is demanded. The total warrior who trusts to the knife for self-defense knows his demeanor must be without passion or fanciful emotion. He will only employ his training and skill when the situation allows for no less, and then he will strike swiftly and with complete commitment.

Japan's greatest swordsman, Miyamoto Musashi, advises the warrior to "approach the enemy with the attitude of defeating him without delay." To accomplish this in a self-defense situation, the warrior must be prepared mentally as well as physically and must understand his weapon, which in this case is the knife. The skilled knife fighter does not dance nor prance nor try to impress his opponent or the crowd with clever techniques. Instead, he closes the gap with sure footwork and deals the least amount of strikes necessary to stop the attack.

Knife training for its intended purpose is deadly serious business and requires the highest order of understanding and self-control. As I have mentioned earlier, both the knife and its skilled use can be misused, but this is true of any thing human beings come into contact with. To fault the instrument or the teachings is simplistic and often a ruse meant to mask far deeper problems in one's society.

Sensei Richard Heckler is a former recon Marine whose martial background includes several fighting systems, including kali. He is a respected aikido instructor and author of *In Search of the Warrior Spirit*. A terrific friend and valued advisor to the author. (Credit: FC archives)

Often warriors are born, but more often they appear on a moment's notice when abuse such as torture, murder, or rape rears its ugly head. These warriors are the common man or woman whose lives are benign in terms of "warrior spirit" or the warrior ethos. In such cases, the training of their skills is centered on simple self-defense using the most effective methods and tools. The knife, wielded by such citizen-warriors, is truly a life saver as opposed to a life taker.

Respect the knife, respect yourself, and respect Life.